# Campbell's
# Low-Fat COOKING

This edition is a revised and enlarged version of the soft-cover *Campbell's Low-Fat Cooking*.



*Campbell's Low-Fat Cooking* was produced by the Publishing Division of Campbell Soup Company, Campbell Place, Camden, NJ 08103-1799.

**Senior Managing Editor:** Pat Teberg
**Assistant Editors:** Ginny Gance, Peg Romano
**Marketing Managers:** Debbie Berkowitz, Kelly Ford, Jill Galowitz, Mike Senackerib
**Consumer Food Center:** Peggy Apice, Dotti Farley, Jane Freiman
**Nutrition Science:** Carole Dichter, D.Sc., R.D.; Patricia Locket, M.S., R.D.
**Photography:** Campbell Creative Photography
Peter Walters Photography/Chicago
Sacco Productions Limited/Chicago

Designed and published by Meredith Publishing Services, 1912 Grand Avenue, Des Moines, IA 50309-3379. Manufactured in U.S.A.

**Pictured on the front cover:** Lemon Thyme Chicken Crunch (*page 30*).

**Preparation and Cooking Times:** Every recipe was developed and tested in the Campbell's Consumer Food Center by professional home economists. Use "Chill Time," "Cook Time," "Marinating Time," "Prep Time," "Stand Time" and/or "Thaw Time" given with each recipe as guides. The preparation times are based on the approximate amount of time required to assemble the recipes *before* baking or cooking. These times include preparation steps, such as chopping; mixing; cooking rice, pasta, vegetables; etc. The fact that some preparation steps can be done simultaneously or during cooking is taken into account. The cook times are based on the minimum amount of time required to cook, bake or broil the food in the recipes.

**Recipe and Nutrition Values:** Values are approximate; calculations are based upon food composition data in the Campbell Soup Company Master Data Base. Some variation in nutrition values may result from periodic product changes.

# Campbell's Low-Fat COOKING


**Smart and Sensible Eating with Campbell's** 4
Handy reference guide featuring the Food Guide Pyramid and the new food label plus low-fat eating tips and sample meal plans—

**Favorites Fit for the Family** 10
Quick-and-easy mealtime solutions featuring chicken, beef and pasta recipes the whole family will enjoy—

**Suppers on the Low-Fat Track** 20
A delicious collection of easy pasta, poultry, pork, beef and fish entrées that are big on taste and low in fat—

**Snappy Soups & Sandwiches** 54
Eat smart anytime with these exciting soups and sandwiches that offer plenty of variety when eaten together or on their own—

**Get-in-Shape Salads & Sides** 72
Perk up everyday or entertaining menus with these contemporary salads, vegetables and pasta side dishes—

**Sensibly Delicious Snacks** 84
Look here for a smart selection of low-fat beverages, snacks and sweets featuring several convenient Campbell products—

**Index** 94

# Smart and Sensible Eating

Limiting dietary fat is one of today's principal nutrition concerns. Health experts believe that most American diets are too high in fat, especially saturated fat. The new Food Guide Pyramid shown below emphasizes foods that are good sources of nutrients and are relatively low in fat. The recipes featured in this new cookbook, *Campbell's Low-Fat Cooking*, were developed to fit in with current dietary recommendations and help people eat "the Pyramid way." Nutrition information is included with the recipes along with the number of Pyramid servings from each food group. Also included are tips that can make low-fat selections almost automatic. These delicious fat- controlled recipes will help you prepare lower-fat meals that are nutritious and tasty as well as quick and easy!

The Food Guide Pyramid outlines how to plan a healthy diet. It calls for eating a variety of foods and, at the same time, the right amount of calories to maintain a healthy weight.

The Pyramid shows how to build your diet from the ground up!

- Start with plenty of foods from the bread, cereals, rice and pasta group and the vegetable and fruit groups.
- Add 2-3 servings from the milk, yogurt and cheese group and 2-3 servings from the meat group (a total of 5-7 ounces per day). Take care to choose lower-fat alternatives—skim, low- and reduced-fat dairy products, lean meat, skinless poultry—most often.

## The Food Guide Pyramid*

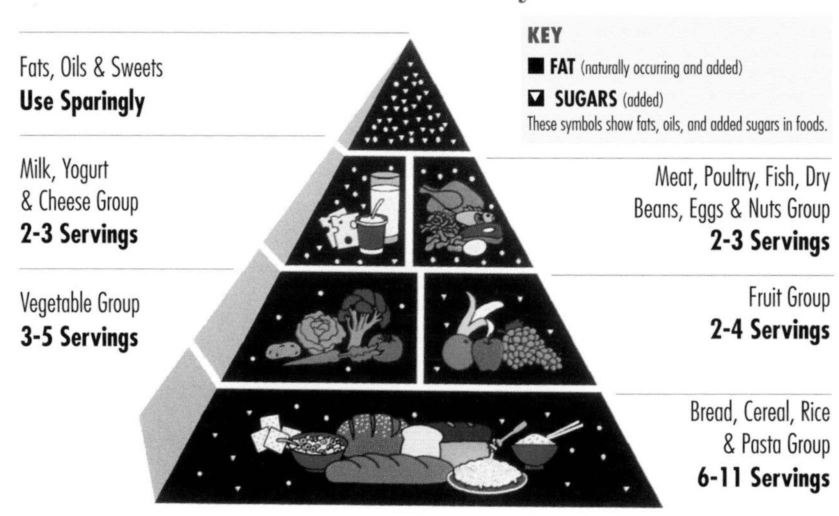


*Source: U. S. Department of Agriculture/Human Nutrition Information Service, Home and Garden Bulletin Number 252. A more detailed description of the Food Guide Pyramid is available by requesting "The Food Guide Pyramid" Bulletin 117-B from the Consumer Information Center, Pueblo, Colorado 81009. Enclose $1.00.

## REMEMBER,

**No one food group is more important than another — all are needed for good health.**

**Go easy on fats, oils and sweets since most foods in this category supply calories but few other nutrients.**

**A range of servings is provided in each food group because individual needs vary with age, sex and activity level.**

**Most people should eat at least the minimum number of servings from each of the five major food groups *every day*.**

## What is a Serving?

**Bread, Cereal, Rice & Pasta Group**
1 slice bread
1 ounce cereal
½ cup rice or pasta

**Vegetable Group**
1 cup raw leafy vegetables
½ cup other vegetables, cooked or chopped raw
¾ cup vegetable juice

**Fruit Group**
1 medium piece of fresh fruit
½ cup chopped, cooked or canned fruit
¾ cup fruit juice

**Milk, Yogurt & Cheese Group**
1 cup milk or yogurt
1½ ounces natural cheese
2 ounces processed cheese

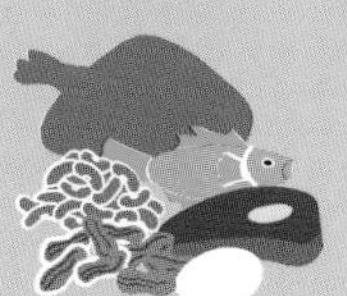

**Meat, Poultry, Fish, Dry Beans, Eggs & Nuts Group**
2-3 ounces cooked lean meat, poultry or fish
½ cup cooked beans or 1 egg or 2 tablespoons of peanut butter = 1 ounce of lean meat

## Sample Diets For a Day at Three Calorie Levels*

| | LOWER (about 1,600 Calories)<br>▲ Sedentary Women<br>▲ Older Adults | MODERATE (about 2,200 Calories)<br>▲ Children<br>▲ Teenage Girls<br>▲ Active Women**<br>▲ Sedentary Men | HIGHER (about 2,800 Calories)<br>▲ Teenage Boys<br>▲ Active Men<br>▲ Very Active Women |
|---|---|---|---|
| Bread Group Servings | 6 | 9 | 11 |
| Vegetable Group Servings | 3 | 4 | 5 |
| Fruit Group Servings | 2 | 3 | 4 |
| Milk Group Servings | 2-3 | 2-3 | 2-3 |
| Meat Group (total ounces) | 5 | 6 | 7 |
| Total Fat (grams) | 53 | 73 | 93 |

**Women who are pregnant or breast-feeding may need more calories.

The chart above lists suggested number of servings at three typical calorie levels that can serve as guidelines to help determine your approximate calorie needs. How many calories you need depends on your age, sex, size and how active you are.

Use the table to estimate how many servings from each group you should be eating and what your maximum daily fat intake should be.

*Source: U.S. Department of Agriculture/Human Nutrition Information Service, Home and Garden Bulletin Number 252.

# The New Nutrition Label

New labels are now appearing on many foods. Look for the heading "Nutrition Facts" to find nutrition information.

**Nutrition Facts**

Serving Size 1 Package (284g)

**Amount Per Serving**

**Calories** 270 Calories from Fat 60

| | % Daily Value* |
|---|---|
| **Total Fat** 7g | **11%** |
| Saturated Fat 3g | **15%** |
| **Cholesterol** 30mg | **10%** |
| **Sodium** 640mg | **27%** |
| **Total Carbohydrate** 35g | **12%** |
| Dietary Fiber 5g | **20%** |
| Sugars 11g | |
| **Protein** 17g | |

Vitamin A 110% • Vitamin C 30%

Calcium 10% • Iron 10%

*Percent Daily Values are based on a 2,000 calorie diet. Your daily values may be higher or lower depending on your calorie needs:

| | Calories | 2,000 | 2,500 |
|---|---|---|---|
| Total Fat | Less than | 65g | 80g |
| Sat Fat | Less than | 20g | 25g |
| Cholesterol | Less than | 300mg | 300mg |
| Sodium | Less than | 2,400mg | 2,400mg |
| Total Carbohydrate | | 300g | 375g |
| Dietary Fiber | | 25g | 30g |

Calories per gram:
Fat 9 • Carbohydrate 4 • Protein 4

**What's different about the new labels?**
There is more information to help plan a healthy daily diet. Note that calories from fat and the amount of total fat and saturated fat are now required on the label.

**How much food is in a serving?**
The new labels give serving sizes in common household measures and also the number of servings per container. You can use the serving size information in the Nutrition Facts panel to determine how much *you* are eating. Be sure to adjust the label information according to the amount you actually eat.

**How can "% Daily Values" be used?**
You can use % Daily Value for "budgeting" nutrients such as fat, saturated fat, cholesterol and sodium. Balance intake of these nutrients over the course of a day or several days.

"% Daily Value" can identify good sources of dietary fiber, vitamins A and C, iron, calcium and other essential vitamins and minerals.

Below are sample menus to illustrate how the recommended number of Pyramid servings fit into a daily meal plan. Nutrition information is also provided to show how the menus fit into an overall healthy diet.

| LOWER (about 1,600 Calories) | MODERATE (about 2,000 Calories) |
|---|---|
| **Breakfast** | **Breakfast** |
| Shredded Wheat cereal (1 oz.) | |
| Wheat toast (1 slice) | Add 1 slice toast |
| Margarine (1 tsp.) | Add jam (1 tbsp.) |
| Banana (1) | |
| Skim milk (8 oz.) | Substitute 2% milk |
| **Lunch** | **Lunch** |
| Nonfat yogurt (8 oz.) | Substitute regular lowfat yogurt |
| Chicken Sandwich: | |
| Wheat bread (2 slices) | |
| "Swanson" Premium Chunk Chicken (2 oz.) | Increase chicken to 3 oz. |
| Lettuce, Tomato | |
| Mayonnaise (1 tsp.) | |
| Apple | |
| **Dinner** | **Dinner** |
| *Beef and Mushrooms Dijon with 1 cup rice | Substitute 1 large roll or add 1 slice bread |
| Broccoli (½ cup) | |
| Small dinner roll or 1 slice bread with margarine (1 tsp.) | |
| **Snacks** | **Snacks** |
| "V8" vegetable juice (5½ oz.) | |
| Orange | Add raisins (1 oz.) |
| **Food Pyramid Servings** | **Food Pyramid Servings** |
| Bread 7 | Bread 9 |
| Fruit 3 | Fruit 4 |
| Vegetable 4 | Vegetable 4 |
| Meat 2 (4 oz.) | Meat 2 (5 oz.) |
| Milk 2 | Milk 2 |

**Calculated Nutrient Values**

| LOWER | | | | MODERATE | | | |
|---|---|---|---|---|---|---|---|
| Calories | 1,618 | Total Diet Fiber,g | 25 | Calories | 1,953 | Total Diet Fiber,g | 30 |
| Total Fat,g | 29 | Total Sugar g | 81 | Total Fat,g | 38 | Total Sugar g | 114 |
| Sat Fat,g | 6 | Protein,g | 79 | Sat Fat,g | 11 | Protein,g | 89 |
| Cholesterol,mg | 98 | Vitamin A,%DV | 104 | Cholesterol,mg | 132 | Vitamin A,%DV | 105 |
| Sodium,mg | 2,137 | Vitamin C,%DV | 367 | Sodium,mg | 2,448 | Vitamin C,%DV | 369 |
| Carbs,g | 265 | Calcium,%DV | 94 | Carbs,g | 322 | Calcium,%DV | 92 |
| ~~*(See recipe, page 46)~~ | | Iron,%DV | 70 | | | Iron,%DV | 83 |

## Low-Fat Cooking Tips from Campbell's

- ▲ Use "Healthy Request" condensed soup as a quick, low-fat sauce (see Easy Lemon Chicken, page 32).
- ▲ Dip chicken into condensed soup before coating with crumb mixtures; bake instead of pan-frying (see Lemon Thyme Chicken Crunch, page 30).
- ▲ Toss cooked pasta with some broth instead of oil to prevent it from sticking together.
- ▲ When making gravy, reduce the amount of drippings to 1 tablespoon. Use 1 can (14½ ounces) broth plus 3 tablespoons flour.
- ▲ Use broth for "stir-frying" instead of oil (see Chicken "Stir-Fry", page 22).
- ▲ For added flavor, use broth instead of water when simmering vegetables, poaching fish or chicken (see Herbed Skillet Vegetables, page 75).
- ▲ Replace butter and milk in mashed potatoes with chicken or vegetable broth.
- ▲ "Healthy Request" tomato soup can be used to replace all or part of the oil in some baked goods (see Cinnamon-Raisin Loaves, page 92).

## Sensible Low-Fat Snacking

- ▲ A cup of "Healthy Request" soup
- ▲ Plain popcorn, without butter or oil
- ▲ Whole grain crackers
- ▲ Unsalted pretzels
- ▲ Low-fat yogurt
- ▲ Unsweetened fruit juice
- ▲ Fruit slices with peels (for more fiber)
- ▲ Tomato or "V8" vegetable juice
- ▲ Cut-up raw vegetables

## A Positive Approach to Healthy Eating

- ▲ Use the Food Pyramid and food label information to help you make healthier food choices.
- ▲ Incorporate changes gradually, making a commitment to a "do-able" eating plan.
- ▲ There are no forbidden foods on a healthy diet.
- ▲ It's your average daily intake that's important.
- ▲ Balancing your food choices over the course of a day or several days will allow you to include a wide variety of foods.

# Favorites Fit for the Family

Variety! If it really is the spice of life, then kids on the go need an extra dash to encourage a well-balanced diet! Exercise their options — and yours — with quick and easy *Barbecued Turkey Pockets, Chicken Broccoli Twist, Corny Mac 'n' Beef, Souperburgers* and *Spicy Cheese Twisters*, all made with versatile Campbell's "Healthy Request" soups. Your whole family will love these low-fat "fast-food" favorites!

Chill-Chasing Chili, top, (page 13) and Chicken Broccoli Twist, bottom, (page 12).

# Chicken Broccoli Twist

3 cups dry corkscrew macaroni
2 cups fresh broccoli flowerets
1 cup sliced carrots (about 2 medium)
1 can (10¾ ounces) CAMPBELL'S HEALTHY REQUEST condensed Cream of Broccoli Soup
1 can (14½ ounces) SWANSON NATURAL GOODNESS Chicken Broth
½ teaspoon garlic powder
⅛ teaspoon pepper
2 cans (5 ounces *each*) SWANSON Premium Chunk White *or* Chunk Chicken, drained
¼ cup grated Parmesan cheese

• In large saucepan prepare macaroni according to package directions, omitting salt. Add broccoli and carrots for last 5 minutes of cooking time. Drain in colander.

• In same pan mix soup, broth, garlic powder, pepper, chicken and macaroni mixture. Over medium heat, heat through, stirring occasionally. Sprinkle with cheese. If desired, garnish with *tomatoes* and *fresh oregano.*

**MAKES 5 SERVINGS • PREP TIME: 10 MINUTES • COOK TIME: 25 MINUTES**

***Nutritional Values Per Serving:*** *Calories 373; Total Fat 5g; Saturated Fat 2g; Cholesterol 33mg; Sodium 698mg; Total Carbohydrate 58g; Protein 23g*
***Food Pyramid Servings:*** *1.5 oz. Meat, Poultry, Fish, Dry Beans, Eggs & Nuts Group; 1¾ servings Bread, Cereal, Rice & Pasta Group; 1 serving Vegetable Group; ¼ serving Milk, Yogurt & Cheese Group*

# Chill-Chasing Chili

- ¾ pound lean ground beef (85% lean)
- ½ cup chopped onion (about 1 medium)
- 1 tablespoon chili powder
- 1 can (10¾ ounces) CAMPBELL'S HEALTHY REQUEST condensed Tomato Soup
- ¼ cup water
- 1 teaspoon vinegar
- 1 can (about 15 ounces) kidney beans, rinsed and drained
- 4 cups hot cooked rice, cooked without salt

• In medium skillet over medium-high heat, cook beef, onion and chili powder until beef is browned, stirring to separate meat. Pour off fat.

• Add soup, water, vinegar and beans. Heat to a boil. Reduce heat to low. Cook 10 minutes. Serve over rice. If desired, garnish with *fresh parsley.*

**MAKES 4 SERVINGS • PREP TIME: 10 MINUTES • COOK TIME: 20 MINUTES**

***Nutritional Values Per Serving:*** *Calories 562; Total Fat 11g; Saturated Fat 4g; Cholesterol 62mg; Sodium 511mg; Total Carbohydrate 83g; Protein 30g*
***Food Pyramid Servings:*** *3.0 oz. Meat, Poultry, Fish, Dry Beans, Eggs & Nuts Group; 2 servings Bread, Cereal, Rice & Pasta Group; ¾ serving Vegetable Group*

# Vegetables 'n' Taters

- 1 can (10¾ ounces) CAMPBELL'S HEALTHY REQUEST condensed Cream of Celery Soup
- ¼ teaspoon dried basil leaves, crushed
- ¼ teaspoon garlic powder
- ⅛ teaspoon pepper
- 1 cup cooked broccoli flowerets
- ½ cup frozen whole kernel corn
- ¾ cup shredded Cheddar cheese (3 ounces)
- 4 hot baked potatoes, split (about 2 pounds)

• In medium saucepan mix soup, basil, garlic powder, pepper, broccoli, corn and *½ cup* cheese. Over medium heat, heat to a boil. Reduce heat to low. Cover and cook 5 minutes or until corn is tender, stirring occasionally.

• Serve over potatoes. Top with remaining cheese.

**MAKES 4 SERVINGS • PREP TIME: 10 MINUTES • COOK TIME: 10 MINUTES**

***Nutritional Values Per Serving:*** *Calories 375; Total Fat 9g; Saturated Fat 5g; Cholesterol 24mg; Sodium 455mg; Total Carbohydrate 64g; Protein 13g*
***Food Pyramid Servings:*** *1¾ servings Vegetable Group; ½ serving Milk, Yogurt & Cheese Group*

# Easy Italian Chicken Bake

4 chicken breast halves (about 2 pounds), skinned
1 can (10¾ ounces) CAMPBELL'S HEALTHY REQUEST condensed Tomato Soup
¼ cup water
2 tablespoons vinegar
1 teaspoon Italian seasoning *or* dried oregano leaves, crushed
½ teaspoon garlic powder
½ cup shredded mozzarella cheese (2 ounces)

• Place chicken in 2-quart shallow baking dish and bake at 375°F. for 30 minutes.

• In small bowl mix soup, water, vinegar, Italian seasoning and garlic powder. Spoon over chicken and bake 25 minutes more. Sprinkle chicken with cheese. Bake 5 minutes more or until chicken is no longer pink. Remove chicken. Stir sauce. If desired, garnish with *fresh oregano.*

**MAKES 4 SERVINGS • PREP TIME: 10 MINUTES • COOK TIME: 1 HOUR**

***Nutritional Values Per Serving:*** *Calories 240; Total Fat 7g; Saturated Fat 3g; Cholesterol 84mg; Sodium 396mg; Total Carbohydrate 12g; Protein 30g*
***Food Pyramid Servings:*** *3.0 oz. Meat, Poultry, Fish, Dry Beans, Eggs & Nuts Group; ½ serving Vegetable Group; ⅓ serving Milk, Yogurt & Cheese Group*

# Corny Mac 'n' Beef

¾ pound lean ground beef (85% lean)
¼ cup chopped onion (about 1 small)
½ teaspoon Italian seasoning *or* dried oregano leaves, crushed
1 can (10¾ ounces) CAMPBELL'S HEALTHY REQUEST condensed Tomato Soup
¼ cup water
1 cup frozen whole kernel corn
3 cups cooked corkscrew macaroni (about 2½ cups dry), cooked without salt
¼ cup grated Parmesan cheese

• In medium skillet over medium-high heat, cook beef, onion and Italian seasoning until beef is browned, stirring to separate meat. Pour off fat.

• Add soup, water and corn. Heat to a boil. Reduce heat to low. Cover and cook 5 minutes or until corn is tender. Add macaroni and heat through. Sprinkle with cheese.

**MAKES 6 SERVINGS • PREP TIME: 10 MINUTES • COOK TIME: 20 MINUTES**

***Nutritional Values Per Serving:*** *Calories 284; Total Fat 9g; Saturated Fat 3g; Cholesterol 44mg; Sodium 275mg; Total Carbohydrate 34g; Protein 18g*
***Food Pyramid Servings:*** *1.5 oz. Meat, Poultry, Fish, Dry Beans, Eggs & Nuts Group; 1 serving Bread, Cereal, Rice & Pasta Group; ¾ serving Vegetable Group*



Easy Italian Chicken Bake

## Spicy Cheese Twisters

- 1 can (10¾ ounces) CAMPBELL'S HEALTHY REQUEST condensed Cream of Chicken Soup
- ½ cup milk (2% fat)
- ⅓ cup cubed pasteurized process cheese spread with jalapeño pepper (3 ounces)
- 3 cups hot cooked corkscrew macaroni (about 2½ cups dry), cooked without salt

• In medium saucepan mix soup, milk and cheese. Over low heat, heat until cheese is melted, stirring often. Toss with macaroni. If desired, garnish with *fresh parsley.*

**MAKES 4 SERVINGS • PREP TIME: 10 MINUTES • COOK TIME: 15 MINUTES**

***Nutritional Values Per Serving:*** *Calories 260; Total Fat 6g; Saturated Fat 3g; Cholesterol 19mg; Sodium 610mg; Total Carbohydrate 40g; Protein 11g*
***Food Pyramid Servings:*** *1½ servings Bread, Cereal, Rice & Pasta Group; ½ serving Milk, Yogurt & Cheese Group*

For a mellow cheese flavor, use plain pasteurized process cheese.

## Honey-Barbecued Chicken

- 1 can (10¾ ounces) CAMPBELL'S condensed Tomato Soup
- 2 tablespoons honey
- 1 teaspoon dry mustard
- ½ teaspoon onion powder
- 4 chicken breast halves (about 2 pounds), skinned

• Mix soup, honey, mustard and onion powder. Place chicken on rack in broiler pan. Broil 6 inches from heat 30 minutes or until chicken is no longer pink, turning and brushing often with soup mixture.

**MAKES 4 SERVINGS • PREP TIME: 10 MINUTES • COOK TIME: 30 MINUTES**

***Nutritional Values Per Serving:*** *Calories 232; Total Fat 4g; Saturated Fat 1g; Cholesterol 73mg; Sodium 513mg; Total Carbohydrate 20g; Protein 28g*
***Food Pyramid Servings:*** *3.0 oz. Meat, Poultry, Fish, Dry Beans, Eggs & Nuts Group; ½ serving Vegetable Group*

# Barbecued Turkey Pockets

- 1 can (10¾ ounces) CAMPBELL'S HEALTHY REQUEST condensed Tomato Soup
- ¼ cup water
- 2 tablespoons packed brown sugar
- 2 tablespoons vinegar
- 1 tablespoon Worcestershire sauce
- 1 pound thinly sliced cooked turkey breast
- 3 pita breads (6 inches *each*), cut in half, forming 2 pockets

• In medium skillet mix soup, water, sugar, vinegar and Worcestershire sauce. Over medium heat, heat to a boil. Reduce heat to low and cook 5 minutes.

• Add turkey and heat through. Spoon *½ cup* turkey mixture into each pita half. If desired, garnish with *fresh fruit.*

**MAKES 6 SERVINGS • PREP TIME: 10 MINUTES • COOK TIME: 15 MINUTES**

***Nutritional Values Per Serving:*** *Calories 242; Total Fat 2g; Saturated Fat 0g; Cholesterol 63mg; Sodium 427mg; Total Carbohydrate 29g; Protein 26g*
***Food Pyramid Servings:*** *2.5 oz. Meat, Poultry, Fish, Dry Beans, Eggs & Nuts Group; 1 serving Bread, Cereal, Rice & Pasta Group; ⅓ serving Vegetable Group*

# Souperburgers

- ¾ pound lean ground beef (85% lean)
- ½ cup chopped onion (about 1 medium)
- 1 can (10¾ ounces) CAMPBELL'S HEALTHY REQUEST condensed Cream of Celery Soup
- ¼ cup water
- 1 tablespoon ketchup
- ⅛ teaspoon pepper
- 6 hamburger rolls, split and toasted

• In medium skillet over medium-high heat, cook beef and onion until beef is browned, stirring to separate meat. Pour off fat.

• Add soup, water, ketchup and pepper. Reduce heat to low and heat through. Spoon *½ cup* meat mixture on each roll.

**MAKES 6 SERVINGS • PREP TIME: 10 MINUTES • COOK TIME: 15 MINUTES**

***Nutritional Values Per Serving:*** *Calories 269; Total Fat 9g; Saturated Fat 4g; Cholesterol 39mg; Sodium 500mg; Total Carbohydrate 28g; Protein 16g*
***Food Pyramid Servings:*** *1.5 oz. Meat, Poultry, Fish, Dry Beans, Eggs & Nuts Group; 2 servings Bread, Cereal, Rice & Pasta Group*

# Suppers on the Low-Fat Track

Even when the schedule squeeze is on, preparing low-fat recipes with big-time taste doesn't have to mean high drama in your kitchen! All you've got to do is act naturally — with "Swanson Natural Goodness" broth! Set the stage for a main event in minutes with mouthwatering *Chicken "Stir-Fry"* or *Honey-Mustard Chicken*. And, when you serve *Lemon Thyme Chicken Crunch* or *Herbed Chicken Vegetable Sauté* to family or dinner guests, you'll discover how cooking with savory Campbell's "Healthy Request" soups means a long run of command performances at your house!

Chicken "Stir-Fry", top, (page 22) and Piquant Pot Roast, bottom, (page 23).

# Chicken "Stir-Fry"

- 2 tablespoons cornstarch
- 1 can (14½ ounces) SWANSON NATURAL GOODNESS Chicken Broth
- 1 tablespoon soy sauce
- 1 pound skinless, boneless chicken breasts, cut into strips
- 4 cups cut-up vegetables (snow peas, celery, carrots *and/or* sweet red pepper)
- ½ teaspoon garlic powder
- ½ teaspoon ground ginger
- 4 cups hot cooked rice, cooked without salt

• In small bowl mix cornstarch, *1½ cups* broth and soy sauce until smooth. Set aside.

• In medium skillet over medium-high heat, heat remaining broth. Add chicken in 2 batches and cook until no longer pink, stirring often. Set chicken aside.

• Add vegetables, garlic powder and ginger. Heat to a boil. Reduce heat to low. Cover and cook 5 minutes or until vegetables are tender-crisp.

• Stir cornstarch mixture and add. Cook until mixture boils and thickens, stirring constantly. Return chicken to pan and heat through. Serve over rice. If desired, garnish with *green onion, celery leaves* and *carrot.*

**MAKES 4 SERVINGS • PREP TIME: 20 MINUTES • COOK TIME: 25 MINUTES**

***Nutritional Values Per Serving:*** *Calories 443; Total Fat 4g; Saturated Fat 1g; Cholesterol 70mg; Sodium 639mg; Total Carbohydrate 66g; Protein 33g*
***Food Pyramid Servings:*** *3.0 oz. Meat, Poultry, Fish, Dry Beans, Eggs & Nuts Group; 2 servings Bread, Cereal, Rice & Pasta Group; 2 servings Vegetable Group*

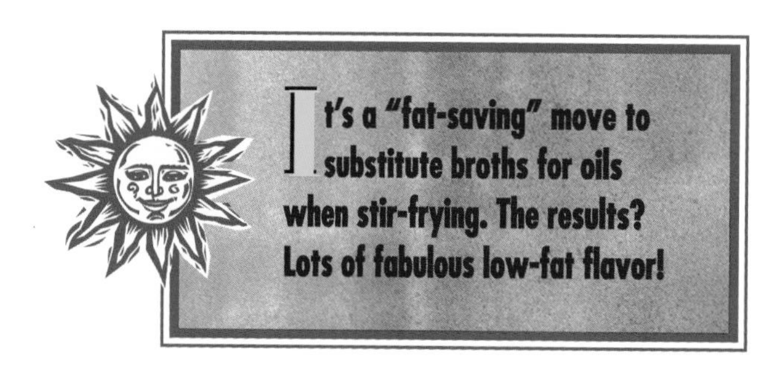

**It's a "fat-saving" move to substitute broths for oils when stir-frying. The results? Lots of fabulous low-fat flavor!**

# Piquant Pot Roast

Vegetable cooking spray
4-pound boneless beef bottom round roast
2 cups V8 Vegetable Juice
¼ teaspoon pepper
⅛ teaspoon garlic powder *or* 1 clove garlic, minced
6 cups potatoes cut in quarters (about 2 pounds)
3 cups carrots cut in 2-inch pieces (about 1 pound)
2 cups onions cut in wedges (about 2 medium)
2 tablespoons all-purpose flour

• Spray Dutch oven with cooking spray and heat over medium-high heat 1 minute. Add roast and cook until browned.

• Add *1¾ cups* "V8" juice, pepper and garlic powder. Heat to a boil. Reduce heat to low. Cover and cook 1 hour 45 minutes, turning roast occasionally.

• Add potatoes, carrots and onions. Cover and cook 45 minutes or until roast is fork-tender, stirring occasionally.

• Transfer roast and vegetables to platter. In cup stir together flour and remaining "V8" juice until smooth. Stir into Dutch oven. Cook over medium heat until mixture boils and thickens, stirring constantly. Serve with roast and vegetables. If desired, garnish with *fresh rosemary.*

**MAKES 12 SERVINGS • PREP TIME: 5 MINUTES • COOK TIME: 2 HOURS 45 MINUTES**

***Nutritional Values Per Serving:*** *Calories 272; Total Fat 8g; Saturated Fat 3g; Cholesterol 68mg; Sodium 178mg; Total Carbohydrate 22g; Protein 28g*
***Food Pyramid Servings:*** *3.5 oz. Meat, Poultry, Fish, Dry Beans, Eggs & Nuts Group; 2 servings Vegetable Group*

**The Food Pyramid recommends a total of about 5 to 7 ounces of poultry, lean meat or fish each day. You don't need big portions — a 3 ounce cooked serving is about the size of a deck of cards.**

# Chicken Primavera

- 2 tablespoons cornstarch
- 1 can (14½ ounces) SWANSON Chicken Broth
- 2 cups fresh broccoli flowerets
- 1 cup sliced carrots (about 2 medium)
- ½ cup sweet red *or* green pepper cut in 2-inch-long strips
- ¼ cup chopped onion (about 1 small)
- 2 cans (5 ounces *each*) SWANSON Premium Chunk White *or* Chunk Chicken, drained
- 4 cups hot cooked spaghetti (about 8 ounces dry), cooked without salt

• In cup mix cornstarch and *¼ cup* broth until smooth. Set aside.

• In medium saucepan mix remaining broth, broccoli, carrots, pepper and onion. Over medium-high heat, heat to a boil. Reduce heat to low. Cover and cook 10 minutes or until vegetables are tender.

• Stir cornstarch mixture and add. Cook until mixture boils and thickens, stirring constantly. Add chicken and heat through. Serve over spaghetti. If desired, sprinkle with *shredded Parmesan cheese.*

**MAKES 4 SERVINGS • PREP TIME: 15 MINUTES • COOK TIME: 20 MINUTES**

***Nutritional Values Per Serving:*** *Calories 338; Total Fat 4g; Saturated Fat 1g; Cholesterol 36mg; Sodium 667mg; Total Carbohydrate 54g; Protein 22g*
***Food Pyramid Servings:*** *2.0 oz. Meat, Poultry, Fish, Dry Beans, Eggs & Nuts Group; 2 servings Bread, Cereal, Rice & Pasta Group; 1¾ servings Vegetable Group*

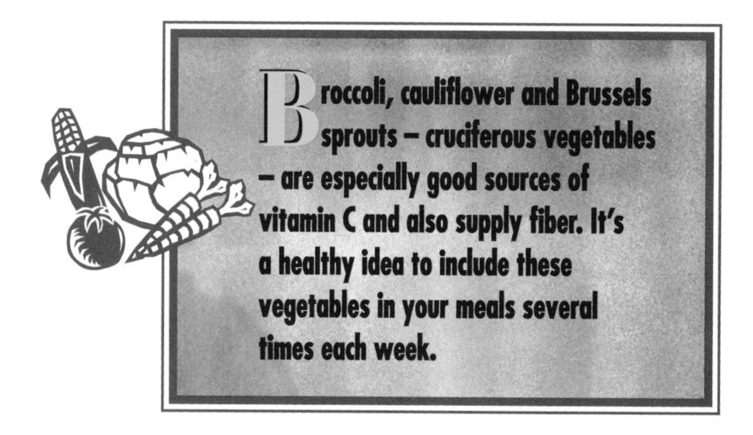

## Savory Lemon Chicken

Vegetable cooking spray
4 skinless, boneless chicken breast halves (about 1 pound)
1 can (10¾ ounces) CAMPBELL'S HEALTHY REQUEST condensed Cream of Chicken Soup
2 tablespoons water
¼ cup chopped sweet red *or* green pepper
1 tablespoon chopped fresh parsley *or* 1 teaspoon dried parsley flakes
1 tablespoon lemon juice
½ teaspoon paprika

• Spray medium skillet with cooking spray and heat over medium-high heat 1 minute. Add chicken and cook 10 minutes or until browned. Set chicken aside.

• Add soup, water, pepper, parsley, lemon juice and paprika. Heat to a boil. Return chicken to pan. Reduce heat to low. Cover and cook 5 minutes or until chicken is no longer pink. If desired, garnish with *lemon slices* and *fresh oregano.*

**MAKES 4 SERVINGS • PREP TIME: 10 MINUTES • COOK TIME: 20 MINUTES**

***Nutritional Values Per Serving:*** *Calories 193; Total Fat 5g; Saturated Fat 1g; Cholesterol 72mg; Sodium 398mg; Total Carbohydrate 8g; Protein 28g*
***Food Pyramid Servings:*** *3.0 oz. Meat, Poultry, Fish, Dry Beans, Eggs & Nuts Group*

## Italian Chicken and Shells

1 tablespoon vegetable oil
4 skinless, boneless chicken breast halves (about 1 pound)
1 can (14½ ounces) SWANSON Chicken Broth
1 teaspoon dried oregano leaves, crushed
½ teaspoon garlic powder
1 can (14½ ounces) whole peeled tomatoes, cut up
1 cup green pepper cut in 2-inch-long strips (about 1 small)
1 cup onion cut in wedges (about 1 medium)
2½ cups dry medium shell macaroni

• In medium skillet over medium-high heat, heat oil. Add chicken and cook 10 minutes or until browned. Set chicken aside. Pour off fat.

• Add broth, oregano, garlic powder, tomatoes, pepper and onion. Heat to a boil. Stir in macaroni. Reduce heat to low. Cover and cook 10 minutes, stirring often.

• Return chicken to pan. Cover and cook 5 minutes or until chicken is no longer pink.

**MAKES 4 SERVINGS • PREP TIME: 10 MINUTES • COOK TIME: 30 MINUTES**

***Nutritional Values Per Serving:*** *Calories 469; Total Fat 8g; Saturated Fat 2g; Cholesterol 73mg; Sodium 678mg; Total Carbohydrate 59g; Protein 37g*
***Food Pyramid Servings:*** *3.0 oz. Meat, Poultry, Fish, Dry Beans, Eggs & Nuts Group; 1¾ servings Bread, Cereal, Rice & Pasta Group; 1¾ servings Vegetable Group*

# Spicy Barbecued Chicken

- 4 chicken breast halves (about 2 pounds), skinned
- 1 can (10¾ ounces) CAMPBELL'S HEALTHY REQUEST condensed Tomato Soup
- 2 tablespoons packed brown sugar
- 3 tablespoons vinegar
- 1 tablespoon Worcestershire sauce
- ¼ teaspoon garlic powder
- 2 teaspoons Louisiana-style hot sauce (optional)
- 4 cups hot cooked rice, cooked without salt

• Place chicken in 2-quart shallow baking dish and bake at 375°F. for 30 minutes.

• Mix soup, sugar, vinegar, Worcestershire sauce, garlic powder and hot sauce. Spoon over chicken and bake 30 minutes more or until chicken is no longer pink. Remove chicken. Stir sauce. Serve with rice. If desired, garnish with *celery leaves* and *green onion.*

**MAKES 4 SERVINGS • PREP TIME: 10 MINUTES • COOK TIME: 1 HOUR**

***Nutritional Values Per Serving:*** *Calories 469; Total Fat 5g; Saturated Fat 1g; Cholesterol 73mg; Sodium 426mg; Total Carbohydrate 71g; Protein 33g*
***Food Pyramid Servings:*** *3.0 oz. Meat, Poultry, Fish, Dry Beans, Eggs & Nuts Group; 2 servings Bread, Cereal, Rice & Pasta Group; ½ serving Vegetable Group*

# Herbed Chicken Vegetable Sauté

- Vegetable cooking spray
- 4 skinless, boneless chicken breast halves (about 1 pound)
- 1 cup fresh broccoli flowerets
- 1 cup sliced fresh mushrooms (about 3 ounces)
- ½ cup very thinly sliced carrot (about 1 medium)
- 1 can (10¾ ounces) CAMPBELL'S HEALTHY REQUEST condensed Cream of Broccoli Soup
- ¾ cup milk (2% fat)
- ¼ teaspoon dried thyme leaves, crushed

• Spray medium skillet with cooking spray and heat over medium-high heat 1 minute. Add chicken and cook 10 minutes or until browned. Set chicken aside.

• Reduce heat to medium. Remove pan from heat. Spray with cooking spray. Add broccoli, mushrooms and carrot and cook until tender-crisp.

• Add soup, milk and thyme. Heat to a boil. Return chicken to pan. Reduce heat to low. Cover and cook 5 minutes or until chicken is no longer pink.

**MAKES 4 SERVINGS • PREP TIME: 15 MINUTES • COOK TIME: 25 MINUTES**

***Nutritional Values Per Serving:*** *Calories 224; Total Fat 6g; Saturated Fat 2g; Cholesterol 77mg; Sodium 366mg; Total Carbohydrate 12g; Protein 31g*
***Food Pyramid Servings:*** *3.0 oz. Meat, Poultry, Fish, Dry Beans, Eggs & Nuts Group; 1¼ servings Vegetable Group*

# Lemon Thyme Chicken Crunch

1 can (10¾ ounces) CAMPBELL'S HEALTHY REQUEST condensed Cream of Chicken Soup
¼ cup water
1 tablespoon lemon juice
⅛ teaspoon dried thyme *or* basil leaves, crushed
⅔ cup dry bread crumbs
¼ teaspoon paprika
4 chicken breast halves (about 2 pounds), skinned
Vegetable cooking spray (optional)

- In small saucepan mix soup, water, lemon juice and thyme. Remove *½ cup* and pour into shallow bowl and set aside.
- Mix crumbs and paprika on plate. Dip chicken into *½ cup* soup mixture. Coat with crumb mixture.
- Place chicken on baking sheet. Spray chicken with cooking spray. Bake at 375°F. for 1 hour or until chicken is no longer pink.
- Heat remaining soup mixture. Serve with chicken. If desired, garnish with *lemon slices.*

**Makes 4 servings • Prep Time: 15 minutes • Cook Time: 1 hour**

***Nutritional Values Per Serving:*** *Calories 264; Total Fat 6g; Saturated Fat 2g; Cholesterol 77mg; Sodium 527mg; Total Carbohydrate 21g; Protein 30g*
***Food Pyramid Servings:*** *3.0 oz. Meat, Poultry, Fish, Dry Beans, Eggs & Nuts Group; ⅓ serving Bread, Cereal, Rice & Pasta Group*

# Herb Broiled Chicken

1 can (10½ ounces) CAMPBELL'S condensed Chicken Broth
3 tablespoons lemon juice
1 teaspoon dried basil leaves, crushed
1 teaspoon dried thyme leaves, crushed
⅛ teaspoon pepper
2 pounds chicken parts

- Mix broth, lemon juice, basil, thyme and pepper and set aside.
- Place chicken on rack in broiler pan. Broil 6 inches from heat 30 minutes or until chicken is no longer pink, turning and brushing often with broth mixture.

**Makes 4 servings • Prep Time: 10 minutes • Cook Time: 30 minutes**

***Nutritional Values Per Serving:*** *Calories 230; Total Fat 9g; Saturated Fat 3g; Cholesterol 96mg; Sodium 563mg; Total Carbohydrate 2g; Protein 33g*
***Food Pyramid Servings:*** *3.0 oz. Meat, Poultry, Fish, Dry Beans, Eggs & Nuts Group*

# Easy Lemon Chicken

Vegetable cooking spray
1 pound skinless, boneless chicken breasts, cut into strips
1 can (10¾ ounces) CAMPBELL'S HEALTHY REQUEST condensed Cream of Broccoli Soup
½ cup milk (2% fat)
2 tablespoons lemon juice
⅛ teaspoon garlic powder
⅛ teaspoon pepper
2 cups cooked broccoli flowerets
4 cups hot cooked rice, cooked without salt

• Spray medium skillet with cooking spray and heat over medium-high heat 1 minute. Add chicken in 2 batches and cook until browned, stirring often. Set chicken aside.

• Add soup, milk, lemon juice, garlic powder, pepper and broccoli. Heat to a boil. Return chicken to pan and heat through. Serve over rice. If desired, garnish with *lemon slices* and *fresh parsley*.

**MAKES 4 SERVINGS • PREP TIME: 15 MINUTES • COOK TIME: 20 MINUTES**

***Nutritional Values Per Serving:*** *Calories 457; Total Fat 8g; Saturated Fat 3g; Cholesterol 65mg; Sodium 366mg; Total Carbohydrate 64g; Protein 30g*
***Food Pyramid Servings:*** *3.0 oz. Meat, Poultry, Fish, Dry Beans, Eggs & Nuts Group; 2 servings Bread, Cereal, Rice & Pasta Group; 1 serving Vegetable Group*

# Chicken Tetrazzini with a Twist

- 3 cups dry corkscrew macaroni
- 1¼ cups shredded zucchini (about 1 medium)
- ½ cup shredded carrot (about 1 medium)
- 1 tablespoon olive oil
- ¼ cup chopped onion (about 1 small)
- 1 can (10¾ ounces) CAMPBELL'S HEALTHY REQUEST condensed Cream of Mushroom Soup
- ¼ cup milk (2% fat)
- ¼ cup low-fat sour cream
- 1 tablespoon grated Parmesan cheese
- 2 cans (5 ounces *each*) SWANSON Premium Chunk White Chicken, drained

• In large saucepan prepare macaroni according to package directions, omitting salt. Add zucchini and carrot for last 1 minute of cooking time. Drain in colander.

• In same pan over medium heat, heat oil. Add onion and cook until tender. Add soup, milk, sour cream, cheese, chicken and macaroni mixture. Heat through, stirring occasionally. If desired, garnish with *carrot flowers* and *fresh oregano.*

**MAKES 4 SERVINGS • PREP TIME: 10 MINUTES • COOK TIME: 25 MINUTES**

***Nutritional Values Per Serving:*** *Calories 477; Total Fat 10g; Saturated Fat 3g; Cholesterol 38mg; Sodium 569mg; Total Carbohydrate 70g; Protein 27g*
***Food Pyramid Servings:*** *2.0 oz. Meat, Poultry, Fish, Dry Beans, Eggs & Nuts Group; 2¼ servings Bread, Cereal, Rice & Pasta Group; 1 serving Vegetable Group*

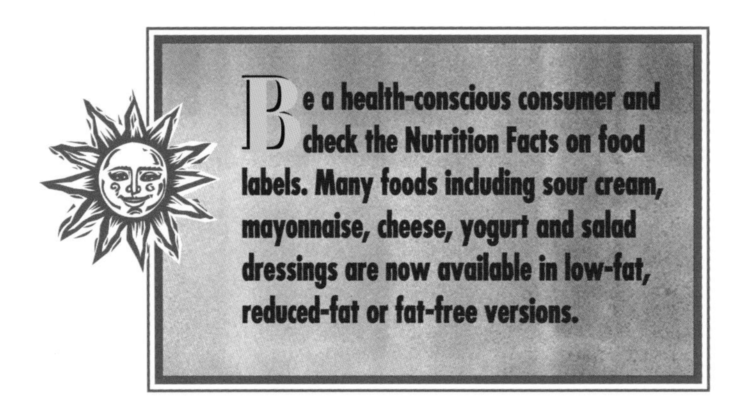

# Herbed Brown Rice and Chicken

- 4 skinless, boneless chicken breast halves (about 1 pound)
- ¼ teaspoon garlic powder
- ⅛ teaspoon pepper
- 1 tablespoon margarine
- 1 can (14½ ounces) SWANSON NATURAL GOODNESS Chicken Broth
- ½ teaspoon dried thyme leaves, crushed
- 1 cup frozen peas
- 1½ cups uncooked quick-cooking brown rice
- 2 tablespoons grated Parmesan cheese

• Sprinkle both sides of chicken with garlic powder and pepper.

• In medium skillet over medium-high heat, heat margarine. Add chicken and cook 10 minutes or until browned. Set chicken aside.

• Stir in broth, thyme, peas and rice. Heat to a boil. Return chicken to pan. Reduce heat to low. Cover and cook 10 minutes or until rice is done and chicken is no longer pink. Remove chicken. Stir cheese into rice mixture. Fluff with fork. If desired, garnish with *fresh thyme, fresh parsley* and *carrots*.

**MAKES 4 SERVINGS • PREP TIME: 5 MINUTES • COOK TIME: 25 MINUTES**

***Nutritional Values Per Serving:*** *Calories 332; Total Fat 8g; Saturated Fat 2g; Cholesterol 75mg; Sodium 474mg; Total Carbohydrate 30g; Protein 34g*
***Food Pyramid Servings:*** *3.0 oz. Meat, Poultry, Fish, Dry Beans, Eggs & Nuts Group; 1½ servings Bread, Cereal, Rice & Pasta Group; ½ serving Vegetable Group*

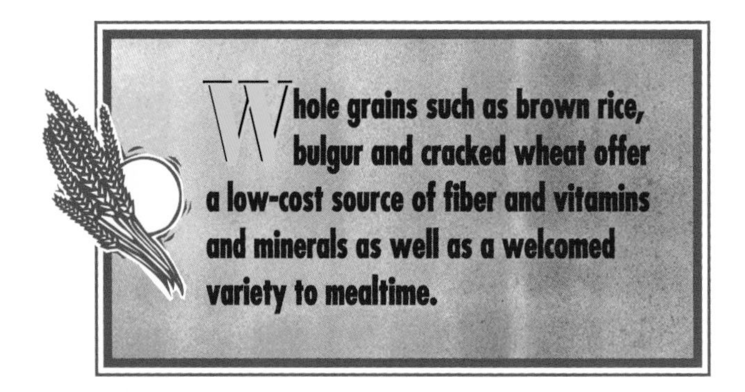

# Skillet Basil Chicken

Vegetable cooking spray
4 skinless, boneless chicken breast halves (about 1 pound)
1 can (10¾ ounces) CAMPBELL'S HEALTHY REQUEST condensed Cream of Mushroom Soup
½ cup milk (2% fat)
1 tablespoon lemon juice
¼ teaspoon dried basil leaves, crushed
⅛ teaspoon garlic powder
1 bag (16 ounces) frozen vegetable combination (broccoli, cauliflower, carrots)

• Spray medium skillet with cooking spray and heat over medium-high heat 1 minute. Add chicken and cook 10 minutes or until browned. Set chicken aside.

• Add soup, milk, lemon juice, basil, garlic powder and vegetables. Heat to a boil. Return chicken to pan. Reduce heat to low. Cover and cook 10 minutes or until chicken is no longer pink.

**MAKES 4 SERVINGS • PREP TIME: 5 MINUTES • COOK TIME: 25 MINUTES**

***Nutritional Values Per Serving:*** *Calories 231; Total Fat 5g; Saturated Fat 2g; Cholesterol 77mg; Sodium 431mg; Total Carbohydrate 14g; Protein 31g*
***Food Pyramid Servings:*** *3.0 oz. Meat, Poultry, Fish, Dry Beans, Eggs & Nuts Group; 1½ servings Vegetable Group*

# Honey-Mustard Chicken

2 tablespoons cornstarch
1 can (14½ ounces) SWANSON NATURAL GOODNESS Clear Chicken Broth
1 tablespoon honey
1 tablespoon Dijon-style mustard
1 tablespoon vegetable oil
4 skinless, boneless chicken breast halves (about 1 pound)
1 cup carrot cut in 2-inch matchstick-thin strips (about 1 large)
½ cup sliced onion (about 1 small)
4 cups hot cooked rice, cooked without salt

• In small bowl mix cornstarch, broth, honey and mustard until smooth. Set aside.

• In nonstick skillet over medium-high heat, heat *half* the oil. Add chicken and cook 10 minutes or until browned. Set chicken aside.

• Reduce heat to medium. Add remaining oil. Add carrot and onion and cook until tender-crisp.

• Stir cornstarch mixture and add. Cook until mixture boils and thickens, stirring constantly. Return chicken to pan. Reduce heat to low. Cook 5 minutes or until chicken is no longer pink. Serve with rice.

**MAKES 4 SERVINGS • PREP TIME: 10 MINUTES • COOK TIME: 25 MINUTES**

***Nutritional Values Per Serving:*** *Calories 477; Total Fat 7g; Saturated Fat 2g; Cholesterol 73mg; Sodium 448mg; Total Carbohydrate 65g; Protein 33g*
***Food Pyramid Servings:*** *3.0 oz. Meat, Poultry, Fish, Dry Beans, Eggs & Nuts Group; 2 servings Bread, Cereal, Rice & Pasta Group; ¾ serving Vegetable Group*



Skillet Basil Chicken

# Italiano Turkey and Pasta

Vegetable cooking spray
1 pound turkey breast cutlets *or* slices, cut into strips
1 jar (27.75 ounces) PREGO EXTRA CHUNKY Garden Combination Spaghetti Sauce (3 cups)
1 tablespoon grated Parmesan cheese
½ teaspoon dried rosemary leaves, crushed
⅛ teaspoon crushed red pepper (optional)
½ cup sliced onion (about 1 medium)
6 cups hot cooked corkscrew macaroni (about 4 cups dry), cooked without salt

• Spray medium skillet with cooking spray and heat over medium-high heat 1 minute. Add turkey in 2 batches and cook until browned, stirring often. Set turkey aside.

• Add spaghetti sauce, cheese, rosemary, pepper and onion. Heat to a boil. Return turkey to pan and heat through. Serve over macaroni. If desired, garnish with *fresh oregano.*

**MAKES 6 SERVINGS • PREP TIME: 10 MINUTES • COOK TIME: 25 MINUTES**

***Nutritional Values Per Serving:*** *Calories 375; Total Fat 3g; Saturated Fat 1g; Cholesterol 51mg; Sodium 532mg; Total Carbohydrate 57g; Protein 27g*
***Food Pyramid Servings:*** *1.5 oz. Meat, Poultry, Fish, Dry Beans, Eggs & Nuts Group; 2 servings Bread, Cereal, Rice & Pasta Group; 1 serving Vegetable Group*

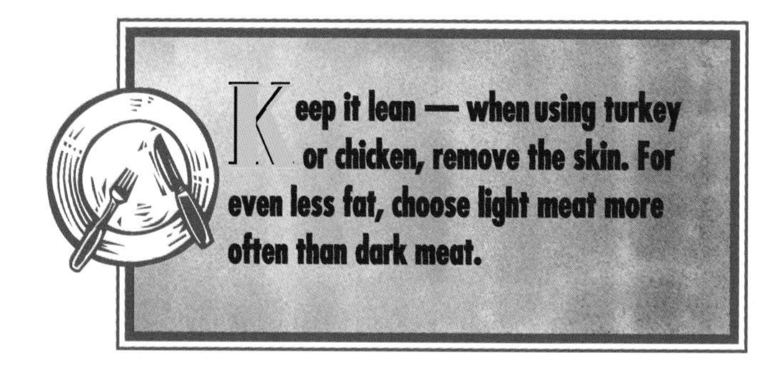

# Broccoli Fish Bake

- 1 package (10 ounces) frozen broccoli spears *or* 1 pound fresh broccoli, cut into spears, cooked and drained
- 1 pound fresh *or* thawed frozen firm white fish fillets (cod, haddock *or* halibut)
- 1 can (10¾ ounces) CAMPBELL'S HEALTHY REQUEST condensed Cream of Broccoli Soup
- ⅓ cup milk (2% fat)
- ¼ cup shredded Cheddar cheese (1 ounce)
- 2 tablespoons dry bread crumbs
- 1 teaspoon margarine, melted
- ⅛ teaspoon paprika

• In 2-quart shallow baking dish, arrange broccoli. Top with fish. In small bowl mix soup and milk and pour over fish.

• Sprinkle cheese over soup mixture. Mix bread crumbs, margarine and paprika and sprinkle over cheese. Bake at 450°F. for 20 minutes or until fish flakes easily when tested with a fork. If desired, garnish with *lemon slices* and *fresh dill.*

**MAKES 4 SERVINGS • PREP TIME: 15 MINUTES • COOK TIME: 20 MINUTES**

***Nutritional Values Per Serving:*** *Calories 212; Total Fat 6g; Saturated Fat 3g; Cholesterol 58mg; Sodium 444mg; Total Carbohydrate 13g; Protein 26g*
***Food Pyramid Servings:*** *3.0 oz. Meat, Poultry, Fish, Dry Beans, Eggs & Nuts Group; ¾ serving Vegetable Group; ¼ serving Milk, Yogurt & Cheese Group*

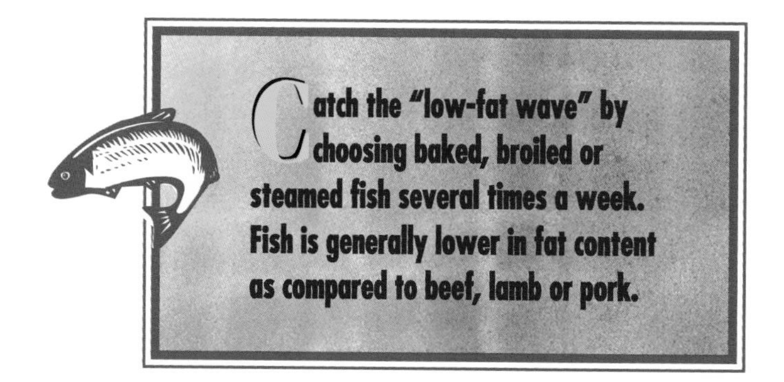

# Shrimp Stir-Fry

- 3 tablespoons cornstarch
- 1 can (14½ ounces) SWANSON NATURAL GOODNESS Chicken Broth
- 1 tablespoon soy sauce
- ½ teaspoon sesame oil (optional)
- 2 tablespoons vegetable oil
- 1 pound medium shrimp, shelled and deveined
- 4 cups cut-up vegetables (asparagus, snow peas *and/or* sweet red, yellow or orange peppers)
- ½ teaspoon ground ginger
- ¼ teaspoon garlic powder *or* 2 cloves garlic, minced
- 4 cups hot cooked rice, cooked without salt

• In small bowl mix cornstarch, broth, soy sauce and sesame oil until smooth. Set aside.

• In medium skillet over medium-high heat, heat *half* the vegetable oil. Add shrimp and stir-fry until pink. Set shrimp aside.

• Reduce heat to medium. Add remaining vegetable oil. Add vegetables, ginger and garlic powder and stir-fry until tender-crisp.

• Stir cornstarch mixture and add. Cook until mixture boils and thickens, stirring constantly. Return shrimp to pan and heat through. Serve over rice.

**MAKES 4 SERVINGS • PREP TIME: 25 MINUTES • COOK TIME: 15 MINUTES**

***Nutritional Values Per Serving:*** *Calories 483; Total Fat 9g; Saturated Fat 2g; Cholesterol 162mg; Sodium 686mg; Total Carbohydrate 72g; Protein 27g*
***Food Pyramid Servings:*** *2.5 oz. Meat, Poultry, Fish, Dry Beans, Eggs & Nuts Group; 2 servings Bread, Cereal, Rice & Pasta Group; 2 servings Vegetable Group*

**Stir-frying is an Oriental cooking technique in which pieces of meat, poultry, seafood and/or vegetables are cooked quickly over high heat with constant stirring. This method requires a minimum amount of fat and results in food that is tender-crisp.**

# Beef and Mushrooms Dijon

¾ pound boneless beef sirloin steak, ¾ inch thick
Vegetable cooking spray
2 cups sliced fresh mushrooms (about 6 ounces)
½ cup sliced onion (about 1 small)
1 can (10¾ ounces) CAMPBELL'S HEALTHY REQUEST condensed Cream of Mushroom Soup
¼ cup water
2 tablespoons Dijon-style mustard
4 cups hot cooked rice, cooked without salt

- Slice beef into very thin strips.
- Spray medium skillet with cooking spray and heat over medium-high heat 1 minute. Add beef and cook until browned. Set beef aside.
- Reduce heat to medium. Remove pan from heat. Spray with cooking spray. Add mushrooms and onion and cook until tender.
- Add soup, water and mustard. Heat to a boil. Return beef to pan and heat through. Serve over rice. If desired, garnish with *fresh sage.*

**MAKES 4 SERVINGS • PREP TIME: 15 MINUTES • COOK TIME: 20 MINUTES**

***Nutritional Values Per Serving:*** *Calories 450; Total Fat 9g; Saturated Fat 3g; Cholesterol 61mg; Sodium 547mg; Total Carbohydrate 61g; Protein 26g*
***Food Pyramid Servings:*** *2.0 oz. Meat, Poultry, Fish, Dry Beans, Eggs & Nuts Group; 2 servings Bread, Cereal, Rice & Pasta Group; 1¼ servings Vegetable Group*

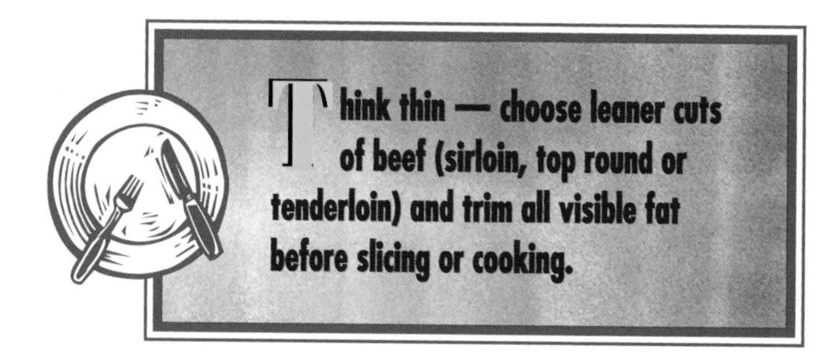

# Beef and Broccoli Stir-Fry

1 pound boneless beef top round steak, ¾ inch thick
2 tablespoons cornstarch
1 can (14½ ounces) SWANSON Beef Broth
1 tablespoon packed brown sugar
1 tablespoon soy sauce
Vegetable cooking spray
¼ teaspoon garlic powder *or* 2 cloves garlic, minced
¼ teaspoon ground ginger
4 cups fresh broccoli flowerets
4 cups hot cooked rice, cooked without salt

• Slice beef into very thin strips. In small bowl mix cornstarch, *1 cup* broth, brown sugar and soy sauce until smooth. Set aside.

• Spray medium skillet with cooking spray and heat over medium-high heat 1 minute. Add beef in 2 batches and stir-fry until browned. Set beef aside.

• Add remaining broth, garlic powder, ginger and broccoli. Heat to a boil. Reduce heat to low. Cover and cook 5 minutes or until broccoli is tender-crisp.

• Stir cornstarch mixture and add. Cook until mixture boils and thickens, stirring constantly. Return beef to pan and heat through. Serve over rice. If desired, garnish with *red pepper flower.*

**MAKES 4 SERVINGS • PREP TIME: 15 MINUTES • COOK TIME: 25 MINUTES**

***Nutritional Values Per Serving:*** *Calories 496; Total Fat 6g; Saturated Fat 2g; Cholesterol 74mg; Sodium 739mg; Total Carbohydrate 71g; Protein 37g*
***Food Pyramid Servings:*** *3.0 oz. Meat, Poultry, Fish, Dry Beans, Eggs & Nuts Group; 2 servings Bread, Cereal, Rice & Pasta Group; 2 servings Vegetable Group*

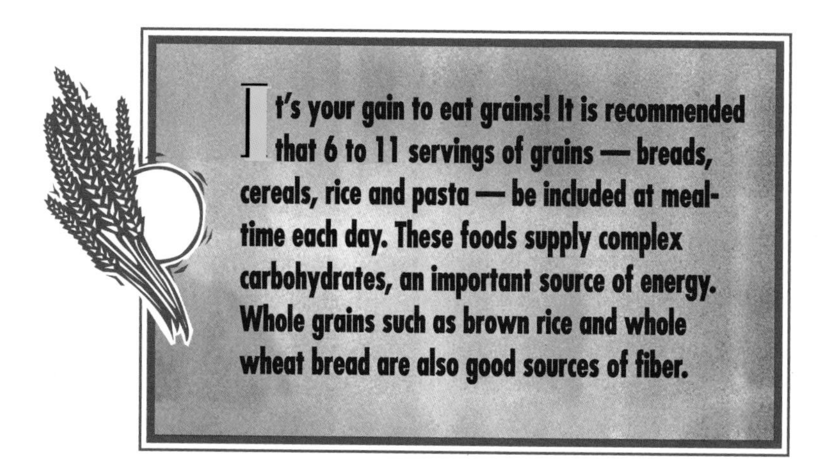

**It's your gain to eat grains! It is recommended that 6 to 11 servings of grains — breads, cereals, rice and pasta — be included at mealtime each day. These foods supply complex carbohydrates, an important source of energy. Whole grains such as brown rice and whole wheat bread are also good sources of fiber.**

# Skillet Beef Oriental

- 1 pound boneless beef sirloin steak, 3/4 inch thick
  Vegetable cooking spray
- 2 cups fresh broccoli flowerets
- 2 cups sliced fresh mushrooms (about 6 ounces)
- 2 cups onions cut in wedges (about 2 medium)
- 1/4 teaspoon garlic powder *or* 2 cloves garlic, minced
- 1 can (10 3/4 ounces) CAMPBELL'S HEALTHY REQUEST condensed Cream of Mushroom Soup
- 1/2 cup water
- 1 tablespoon low-sodium soy sauce
- 4 cups hot cooked rice, cooked without salt

• Slice beef into very thin strips. Spray medium skillet with cooking spray and heat over medium-high heat 1 minute. Add beef in 2 batches and cook until browned, stirring often. Set beef aside.

• Reduce heat to medium. Remove pan from heat. Spray with cooking spray. Add broccoli, mushrooms, onions and garlic powder and cook until tender-crisp. Add soup, water and soy sauce. Heat to a boil. Return beef to pan and heat through. Serve over rice. If desired, garnish with *sweet red pepper.*

**MAKES 4 SERVINGS • PREP TIME: 20 MINUTES • COOK TIME: 25 MINUTES**

***Nutritional Values Per Serving:*** *Calories 457; Total Fat 7g; Saturated Fat 2g; Cholesterol 56mg; Sodium 645mg; Total Carbohydrate 69g; Protein 28g*
***Food Pyramid Servings:*** *3.0 oz. Meat, Poultry, Fish, Dry Beans, Eggs & Nuts Group; 2 servings Bread, Cereal, Rice & Pasta Group; 3 servings Vegetable Group*

# Smothered Pork Chops

- 2 tablespoons cornstarch
- 1 can (14 1/2 ounces) SWANSON Beef Broth
- 1 tablespoon packed brown sugar
  Vegetable cooking spray
- 6 pork chops, 1/2 inch thick (about 1 1/2 pounds)
- 1 cup sliced onion (about 1 medium)
- 6 cups hot cooked egg noodles (about 6 cups dry), cooked without salt

• In small bowl mix cornstarch, broth and brown sugar until smooth. Set aside. Spray medium skillet with cooking spray and heat over medium-high heat 1 minute. Add chops in 2 batches and cook 10 minutes or until browned. Set chops aside.

• Stir cornstarch mixture and add with onion. Cook until mixture boils and thickens, stirring constantly. Return chops to pan. Reduce heat to low. Cover and cook 5 minutes or until chops are no longer pink. Serve with noodles.

**MAKES 6 SERVINGS • PREP TIME: 5 MINUTES • COOK TIME: 30 MINUTES**

***Nutritional Values Per Serving:*** *Calories 417; Total Fat 10g; Saturated Fat 3g; Cholesterol 120mg; Sodium 308mg; Total Carbohydrate 47g; Protein 32g*
***Food Pyramid Servings:*** *2.0 oz. Meat, Poultry, Fish, Dry Beans, Eggs & Nuts Group; 2 servings Bread, Cereal, Rice & Pasta Group; 1/3 serving Vegetable Group*



Skillet Beef Oriental

# Harvest Pork 'n' Noodles

Vegetable cooking spray
4 pork chops, ¾ inch thick (about 1½ pounds)
1 can (10¾ ounces) CAMPBELL'S HEALTHY REQUEST condensed Cream of Celery Soup
¼ cup apple juice *or* water
2 tablespoons spicy brown mustard
1 tablespoon honey
⅛ teaspoon pepper
4 cups hot cooked egg noodles (about 4 cups dry), cooked without salt

• Spray medium skillet with cooking spray and heat over medium-high heat 1 minute. Add chops and cook 10 minutes or until browned. Set aside. Add soup and next 4 ingredients. Heat to a boil. Return chops to pan. Reduce heat to low. Cover and cook 10 minutes or until chops are no longer pink. Serve with noodles. If desired, garnish with *fresh rosemary.*

**MAKES 4 SERVINGS • PREP TIME: 5 MINUTES • COOK TIME: 25 MINUTES**

***Nutritional Values Per Serving:*** *Calories 455; Total Fat 10g; Saturated Fat 3g; Cholesterol 122mg; Sodium 386mg; Total Carbohydrate 52g; Protein 35g*
***Food Pyramid Servings:*** *3.0 oz. Meat, Poultry, Fish, Dry Beans, Eggs & Nuts Group; 2 servings Bread, Cereal, Rice & Pasta Group*

# Quick and Easy Swiss Steak

1 pound boneless beef top round steak, ¾ inch thick
3 tablespoons cornstarch
1 can (14½ ounces) SWANSON Beef Broth
Vegetable cooking spray
½ teaspoon garlic powder
1 cup cut-up canned tomatoes
1 cup onion cut in wedges (about 1 medium)
½ cup sliced celery (about 1 rib)
4 cups hot cooked egg noodles (about 4 cups dry), cooked without salt

• Slice beef into very thin strips. In small bowl mix cornstarch and *1 cup* broth until smooth. Set aside. Spray medium skillet with cooking spray and heat over medium-high heat 1 minute. Add beef in 2 batches and cook until browned. Set beef aside.

• Add remaining broth, garlic powder, tomatoes, onion and celery. Heat to a boil. Reduce heat to low. Cover and cook 5 minutes or until vegetables are tender-crisp.

• Stir cornstarch mixture and add. Cook until mixture boils and thickens, stirring constantly. Return beef to pan and heat through. Serve over noodles.

**MAKES 4 SERVINGS • PREP TIME: 15 MINUTES • COOK TIME: 25 MINUTES**

***Nutritional Values Per Serving:*** *Calories 440; Total Fat 8g; Saturated Fat 3g; Cholesterol 126mg; Sodium 535mg; Total Carbohydrate 52g; Protein 38g*
***Food Pyramid Servings:*** *3.0 oz. Meat, Poultry, Fish, Dry Beans, Eggs & Nuts Group; 2 servings Bread, Cereal, Rice & Pasta Group; 1¼ servings Vegetable Group*



Harvest Pork 'n' Noodles

# Snappy Soups & Sandwiches

The world's favorite comfort food and the pocket passion...The timeless appeal of soup and sandwich is an affair to remember! Whether it's a casual family meal, brown-bag lunch or "big game fare" for your favorite armchair quarterbacks, sensible goes sensational with *Chicken and Bean Burritos, Vegetarian Chili, Barbecued Chicken Sandwiches* and *Hearty Vegetable Soup*. Apart or together, these healthfully zesty soup and sandwich recipes make it so easy to eat smart anytime!

Vegetarian Chili, top, (page 56) and
Zesty Chicken Fajitas, bottom, (page 57).

# Vegetarian Chili

- 1 can (14½ ounces) SWANSON Vegetable Broth
- 1 tablespoon chili powder
- ½ teaspoon dried thyme leaves, crushed
- ⅛ teaspoon pepper
- 2 cups coarsely chopped zucchini (about 2 small)
- 1 can (14½ ounces) whole peeled tomatoes, cut up
- 1 cup chopped carrots (about 2 large)
- 1 can (about 16 ounces) black beans, rinsed and drained
- 1 can (about 16 ounces) chick peas (garbanzo beans), rinsed and drained
- 6 cups hot cooked rice, cooked without salt

• In large saucepan mix broth, chili powder, thyme, pepper, zucchini, tomatoes and carrots. Over medium-high heat, heat to a boil. Reduce heat to low. Cover and cook 20 minutes or until vegetables are tender. Add black beans and chick peas and heat through. Serve with rice. If desired, garnish with *green onion.*

**MAKES ABOUT 8 CUPS OR 6 SERVINGS • PREP TIME: 10 MINUTES • COOK TIME: 30 MINUTES**

***Nutritional Values Per Serving:*** *Calories 423; Total Fat 3g; Saturated Fat 0g; Cholesterol 0mg; Sodium 664mg; Total Carbohydrate 85g; Protein 15g*
***Food Pyramid Servings:*** *1.0 oz. Meat, Poultry, Fish, Dry Beans, Eggs & Nuts Group; 2 servings Bread, Cereal, Rice & Pasta Group; 1¾ servings Vegetable Group*

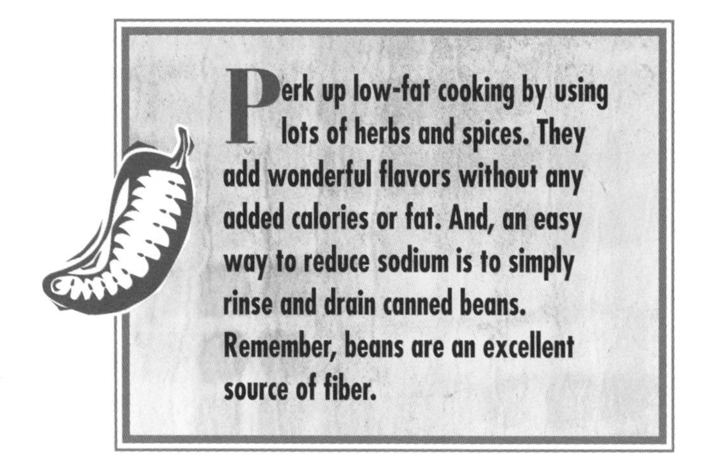

# Zesty Chicken Fajitas

1 cup refrigerated MARIE'S Zesty Fat Free Classic Herb Vinaigrette
2 tablespoons soy sauce
6 skinless, boneless chicken breast halves (about 1½ pounds)
½ cup coarsely chopped onion (about 1 medium)
½ cup chopped tomato (about 1 small)
8 flour tortillas (8 inches *each*)
½ cup shredded Cheddar cheese (2 ounces)
2 cups shredded lettuce

• Mix *½ cup* vinaigrette and soy sauce in shallow nonmetallic dish. Add chicken and turn to coat. Cover and refrigerate 1 hour, turning chicken occasionally.

• Remove chicken from marinade and place on rack in broiler pan. Discard marinade. Broil 4 inches from heat 15 minutes or until chicken is no longer pink, turning once.

• Mix remaining vinaigrette, onion and tomato. Set aside.

• Warm tortillas according to package directions. Slice chicken into thin strips and place ½ cup down center of each tortilla. Top each with 2 tablespoons vinaigrette mixture, 1 tablespoon cheese and ¼ cup lettuce. Fold tortilla around filling. If desired, garnish with *sweet red pepper strips* and *fresh cilantro.*

**Makes 8 servings • Prep Time: 10 minutes • Marinating Time: 1 hour • Cook Time: 15 minutes**

***Nutritional Values Per Serving:*** *Calories 289; Total Fat 7g; Saturated Fat 3g; Cholesterol 63mg; Sodium 766mg; Total Carbohydrate 29g; Protein 25g*
***Food Pyramid Servings:*** *2.0 oz. Meat, Poultry, Fish, Dry Beans, Eggs & Nuts Group; 1 serving Bread, Cereal, Rice & Pasta Group; ½ serving Vegetable Group*

# Creamy Potato Soup

1 can (14½ ounces) SWANSON Chicken Broth
⅛ teaspoon pepper
3 cups peeled potatoes sliced ¼-inch thick (about 1 pound)
½ cup sliced celery (about 1 rib)
½ cup sliced green onions (about 4)
1½ cups milk (2% fat)

• In medium saucepan mix broth, pepper, potatoes, celery and onions. Over medium-high heat, heat to a boil. Reduce heat to low. Cover and cook 15 minutes or until vegetables are tender. Remove from heat.

• In blender or food processor, place *half* the broth mixture and *¾ cup* milk. Blend until smooth. Repeat with remaining broth mixture and remaining milk. Return to pan. Over medium heat, heat through. If desired, garnish with *sweet red pepper strips* and *green onions.*

**MAKES ABOUT 5 CUPS OR 5 SERVINGS • PREP TIME: 15 MINUTES • COOK TIME: 35 MINUTES**

***Nutritional Values Per Serving:*** *Calories 121; Total Fat 2g; Saturated Fat 1g; Cholesterol 6mg; Sodium 406mg; Total Carbohydrate 21g; Protein 5g*
***Food Pyramid Servings:*** *1½ servings Vegetable Group; ¼ serving Milk, Yogurt & Cheese Group*

# Mac 'n' Vegetable Soup

2 cans (14½ ounces *each*) SWANSON Vegetable Broth
½ teaspoon dried basil leaves, crushed
¼ teaspoon garlic powder
1 package (about 9 ounces) frozen mixed vegetables (about 2 cups)
1 can (about 14½ ounces) whole peeled tomatoes, cut up
1 cup dry corkscrew macaroni

• In medium saucepan mix broth, basil, garlic powder, vegetables and tomatoes. Over medium-high heat, heat to a boil. Stir in macaroni. Reduce heat to medium. Cook 15 minutes or until macaroni is done, stirring occasionally.

**MAKES ABOUT 6½ CUPS OR 6 SERVINGS • PREP TIME: 10 MINUTES • COOK TIME: 25 MINUTES**

***Nutritional Values Per Serving:*** *Calories 126; Total Fat 1g; Saturated Fat 0g; Cholesterol 0mg; Sodium 687mg; Total Carbohydrate 25g; Protein 5g*
***Food Pyramid Servings:*** *½ serving Bread, Cereal, Rice & Pasta Group; 1¼ servings Vegetable Group*

# Mexican Chicken Soup

Olive oil *or* vegetable cooking spray
1 pound skinless, boneless chicken breasts, cut into cubes
1 cup coarsely chopped green *or* sweet red pepper (about 1 large)
2 teaspoons chili powder
1 teaspoon garlic powder
2 cans (14½ ounces *each*) SWANSON NATURAL GOODNESS Chicken Broth
1 package (10 ounces) frozen whole kernel corn (about 1¾ cups)
1 cup cooked rice, cooked without salt
1 teaspoon chopped fresh cilantro *or* parsley (optional)
5 lime wedges

• Spray large saucepan with cooking spray and heat over medium heat 1 minute. Add chicken, pepper, chili powder and garlic powder and cook 5 minutes, stirring often.

• Add broth, corn and rice. Heat to a boil. Reduce heat to low. Cook 10 minutes. Stir in cilantro. Serve with lime wedges. If desired, garnish with *fresh cilantro.*

**Makes about 6½ cups or 5 servings • Prep Time: 15 minutes • Cook Time: 20 minutes**

***Nutritional Values Per Serving:*** *Calories 235; Total Fat 4g; Saturated Fat 1g; Cholesterol 56mg; Sodium 514mg; Total Carbohydrate 27g; Protein 25g*
***Food Pyramid Servings:*** *2.0 oz. Meat, Poultry, Fish, Dry Beans, Eggs & Nuts Group; ⅓ serving Bread, Cereal, Rice & Pasta Group; 1 serving Vegetable Group*

# Italian Vegetable Soup

2 cans (14½ ounces *each*) SWANSON NATURAL GOODNESS Chicken Broth
3 cups Low Sodium V8 Vegetable Juice
1½ teaspoons Italian seasoning, crushed
½ teaspoon garlic powder *or* 4 cloves garlic, minced
¼ teaspoon pepper
1 bag (16 ounces) frozen Italian-style vegetable combination
1 can (about 15 ounces) kidney beans, rinsed and drained
2 teaspoons grated Parmesan cheese

• In large saucepan mix broth, "V8" juice, Italian seasoning, garlic powder, pepper and Italian-style vegetables. Over medium-high heat, heat to a boil. Reduce heat to low. Cover and cook 10 minutes or until vegetables are tender. Add beans and cheese and heat through.

**Makes about 8½ cups or 8 servings • Prep Time: 5 minutes • Cook Time: 25 minutes**

***Nutritional Values Per Serving:*** *Calories 120; Total Fat 1g; Saturated Fat 1g; Cholesterol 1mg; Sodium 462mg; Total Carbohydrate 21g; Protein 8g*
***Food Pyramid Servings:*** *0.5 oz. Meat, Poultry, Fish, Dry Beans, Eggs & Nuts Group; 1 serving Vegetable Group*

# Tortellini Soup

2 cans (14½ ounces *each*) SWANSON NATURAL GOODNESS Chicken Broth
⅛ teaspoon pepper
½ cup chopped carrot (about 1 large)
½ cup sliced celery (about 1 rib)
2 ounces frozen cheese-filled tortellini (about ½ cup)
1 tablespoon chopped fresh parsley *or* 1 teaspoon dried parsley flakes

• In medium saucepan mix broth, pepper, carrot and celery. Over medium-high heat, heat to a boil. Add tortellini. Reduce heat to medium. Cook 15 minutes or until tortellini is done, stirring occasionally. Stir in parsley.

**MAKES ABOUT 3¾ CUPS OR 4 SERVINGS • PREP TIME: 10 MINUTES • COOK TIME: 20 MINUTES**

***Nutritional Values Per Serving:*** *Calories 79; Total Fat 2g; Saturated Fat 1g; Cholesterol 9mg; Sodium 656mg; Total Carbohydrate 10g; Protein 5g*
***Food Pyramid Servings:*** *½ serving Vegetable Group*

# Chicken Quesadillas

1 can (10¾ ounces) CAMPBELL'S HEALTHY REQUEST condensed Cream of Chicken Soup
1 teaspoon chili powder
½ cup shredded Cheddar cheese (2 ounces)
2 cans (5 ounces *each*) SWANSON Premium Chunk White *or* Chunk Chicken, drained
8 flour tortillas (8 inches *each*)

• Mix soup, chili powder, cheese and chicken.

• Place tortillas on 2 baking sheets. Top half of each tortilla with about *¼ cup* soup mixture. Spread to within ½ inch of edge. Moisten edges of tortilla with water. Fold over and press edges together.

• Bake at 400°F. for 10 minutes or until hot.

**MAKES 8 SERVINGS • PREP TIME: 15 MINUTES • COOK TIME: 10 MINUTES**

***Nutritional Values Per Serving:*** *Calories 203; Total Fat 7g; Saturated Fat 2g; Cholesterol 27mg; Sodium 464mg; Total Carbohydrate 23g; Protein 12g*
***Food Pyramid Servings:*** *1.0 oz. Meat, Poultry, Fish, Dry Beans, Eggs & Nuts Group; 1 serving Bread, Cereal, Rice & Pasta Group*

# Hearty Tomato Rice Soup

- Vegetable cooking spray
- 1 cup coarsely chopped zucchini (about 1 small)
- ½ teaspoon dried basil leaves, crushed
- ⅛ teaspoon garlic powder *or* 1 clove garlic, minced
- 1 can (10¾ ounces) CAMPBELL'S HEALTHY REQUEST condensed Tomato Soup
- 1 soup can water
- 1 teaspoon lemon juice
- 1½ cups cooked rice, cooked without salt
- 2 tablespoons finely shredded Parmesan cheese

• Spray medium saucepan with cooking spray and heat over medium heat 1 minute. Add zucchini, basil and garlic powder and cook until tender-crisp.

• Add soup, water, lemon juice and rice and heat through. Sprinkle with cheese.

**MAKES ABOUT 4 CUPS OR 4 SERVINGS • PREP TIME: 15 MINUTES • COOK TIME: 10 MINUTES**

***Nutritional Values Per Serving:*** *Calories 165; Total Fat 2g; Saturated Fat 1g; Cholesterol 3mg; Sodium 320mg; Total Carbohydrate 32g; Protein 4g*
***Food Pyramid Servings:*** *¾ serving Bread, Cereal, Rice & Pasta Group; 1 serving Vegetable Group*

# Curried Chicken Chowder

- 1 can (10¾ ounces) CAMPBELL'S HEALTHY REQUEST condensed Cream of Chicken Soup
- 1 can (10¾ ounces) CAMPBELL'S HEALTHY REQUEST condensed Chicken with Rice Soup
- 2 soup cans water
- 1 teaspoon curry powder
- 2 cups potatoes cut in cubes (about 2 medium)
- 1 package (about 9 ounces) frozen mixed vegetables (about 2 cups)
- ¼ cup diced green *or* sweet red pepper
- 2 cans (5 ounces *each*) SWANSON Premium Chunk White *or* Chunk Chicken, drained

• In large saucepan mix soups, water, curry powder, potatoes, vegetables and pepper. Over medium-high heat, heat to a boil. Reduce heat to low. Cover and cook 10 minutes or until vegetables are tender. Add chicken and heat through.

**MAKES ABOUT 8 CUPS OR 6 SERVINGS • PREP TIME: 10 MINUTES • COOK TIME: 20 MINUTES**

***Nutritional Values Per Serving:*** *Calories 176; Total Fat 4g; Saturated Fat 1g; Cholesterol 29mg; Sodium 560mg; Total Carbohydrate 24g; Protein 13g*
***Food Pyramid Servings:*** *1.5 oz. Meat, Poultry, Fish, Dry Beans, Eggs & Nuts Group; 1⅓ servings Vegetable Group*



Hearty Tomato Rice Soup

# Chicken and Broccoli Pockets

1 can (10¾ ounces) CAMPBELL'S HEALTHY REQUEST condensed Cream of Chicken Soup
¼ cup water
1 tablespoon lemon juice
¼ teaspoon garlic powder
⅛ teaspoon pepper
1 cup cooked broccoli flowerets
½ cup shredded carrot (about 1 medium)
2 cups cubed cooked chicken
3 pita breads (6 inches *each*), cut in half, forming 2 pockets

• In medium saucepan mix soup, water, lemon juice, garlic powder, pepper, broccoli, carrot and chicken. Over medium heat, heat through. Spoon ½ *cup* mixture into each pita half. If desired, garnish with *tomatoes* and *fresh parsley*.

**Makes 6 servings • Prep Time: 10 minutes • Cook Time: 10 minutes**

***Nutritional Values Per Serving:*** *Calories 212; Total Fat 5g; Saturated Fat 1g; Cholesterol 38mg; Sodium 420mg; Total Carbohydrate 25g; Protein 17g*
***Food Pyramid Servings:*** *1.5 oz. Meat, Poultry, Fish, Dry Beans, Eggs & Nuts Group; 1 serving Bread, Cereal, Rice & Pasta Group; ½ serving Vegetable Group*

# Barbecued Chicken Sandwiches

Vegetable cooking spray
½ cup chopped green pepper (about 1 small)
¼ cup chopped celery
¼ cup chopped onion (about 1 small)
½ cup bottled barbecue sauce
2 cans (5 ounces *each*) SWANSON Premium Chunk White *or* Chunk Chicken, drained
4 hamburger rolls, split and toasted

• Spray medium saucepan with cooking spray and heat over medium heat 1 minute. Add pepper, celery and onion and cook until tender.

• Add barbecue sauce and chicken. Heat through. Divide chicken mixture evenly among rolls.

**Makes 4 servings • Prep Time: 10 minutes • Cook Time: 10 minutes**

***Nutritional Values Per Serving:*** *Calories 234; Total Fat 5g; Saturated Fat 2g; Cholesterol 35mg; Sodium 702mg; Total Carbohydrate 29g; Protein 17g*
***Food Pyramid Servings:*** *2.0 oz. Meat, Poultry, Fish, Dry Beans, Eggs & Nuts Group; 2 servings Bread, Cereal, Rice & Pasta Group; ½ serving Vegetable Group*



Chicken and Broccoli Pockets

## Hearty Vegetable Soup

- 3 cans (14½ ounces *each*) SWANSON Vegetable Broth
- ½ teaspoon dried basil leaves, crushed
- 2 cups shredded cabbage
- 2 cups zucchini cut in half lengthwise and sliced (about 2 medium)
- 1 package (about 9 ounces) frozen cut green beans (about 2 cups)
- 1½ cups sliced carrots (about 3 medium)
- 1 cup sliced celery (about 2 ribs)
- ¼ cup uncooked regular long-grain rice

• In large saucepan mix broth, basil, cabbage, zucchini, beans, carrots and celery. Over medium-high heat, heat to a boil. Stir in rice. Reduce heat to low. Cover and cook 20 minutes or until rice is done.

**MAKES ABOUT 8 CUPS OR 8 SERVINGS • PREP TIME: 15 MINUTES • COOK TIME: 30 MINUTES**

***Nutritional Values Per Serving:*** *Calories 66; Total Fat 1g; Saturated Fat 0g; Cholesterol 0mg; Sodium 686mg; Total Carbohydrate 14g; Protein 2g*
***Food Pyramid Servings:*** *2 servings Vegetable Group*

## Chicken and Bean Burritos

- Vegetable cooking spray
- ½ cup chopped onion (about 1 medium)
- ¼ teaspoon dried oregano leaves, crushed
- ⅛ teaspoon garlic powder *or* 1 clove garlic, minced
- 1 can (11½ ounces) CAMPBELL'S HEALTHY REQUEST condensed Bean with Bacon Soup
- ¾ cup PACE Thick & Chunky Salsa
- 2 cups chopped cooked chicken
- 8 flour tortillas (8 inches *each*)

• Spray medium skillet with cooking spray and heat over medium heat 1 minute. Add onion, oregano and garlic powder and cook until tender.

• Add soup, salsa and chicken and heat through.

• Warm tortillas according to package directions. Spoon about *⅓ cup* chicken mixture down center of each tortilla. Fold tortilla around filling. If desired, serve with *salad.*

**MAKES 8 SERVINGS • PREP TIME: 10 MINUTES • COOK TIME: 10 MINUTES**

***Nutritional Values Per Serving:*** *Calories 239; Total Fat 6g; Saturated Fat 1g; Cholesterol 27mg; Sodium 648mg; Total Carbohydrate 30g; Protein 14g*
***Food Pyramid Servings:*** *1.0 oz. Meat, Poultry, Fish, Dry Beans, Eggs & Nuts Group; 1 serving Bread, Cereal, Rice & Pasta Group; ½ serving Vegetable Group*

Hearty Vegetable Soup *(top)*
Chicken and Bean Burritos *(bottom)*

# Chicken Salad Sandwiches

- 2 cans (5 ounces *each*) SWANSON Premium Chunk White *or* Chunk Chicken, drained
- ¼ cup chopped celery
- 1 tablespoon finely chopped onion
- ¼ cup nonfat mayonnaise dressing
- ⅛ teaspoon pepper
- 8 slices PEPPERIDGE FARM Whole Wheat Thin Sliced Bread
- 4 tomato slices (about 1 small)
- 4 lettuce leaves

• Mix chicken, celery, onion, mayonnaise and pepper.

• Divide chicken mixture evenly among 4 bread slices. Top with tomato, lettuce and remaining bread slices. If desired, serve with *fresh fruit* and *celery leaves.*

**MAKES 4 SERVINGS • PREP TIME: 10 MINUTES**

***Nutritional Values Per Serving:*** *Calories 215; Total Fat 4g; Saturated Fat 1g; Cholesterol 35mg; Sodium 635mg; Total Carbohydrate 30g; Protein 17g*
***Food Pyramid Servings:*** *2.0 oz. Meat, Poultry, Fish, Dry Beans, Eggs & Nuts Group; 2 servings Bread, Cereal, Rice & Pasta Group; ½ serving Vegetable Group*

# Oriental Chicken Sandwiches

- 1 can (5 ounces) SWANSON Premium Chunk White *or* Chunk Chicken, drained
- ¼ cup green *or* sweet red pepper cut in 2-inch-long strips
- ¼ cup sliced green onions (about 2)
- ¼ cup low-fat sour cream
- ½ teaspoon honey
- ½ teaspoon sesame oil (optional)
- ⅛ teaspoon crushed red pepper
- 4 slices PEPPERIDGE FARM Light Style Wheat Bread
- 4 lettuce leaves

• Mix chicken, pepper, onions, sour cream, honey, oil and crushed red pepper.

• Divide chicken mixture evenly between 2 bread slices. Top with lettuce and remaining bread slices.

**MAKES 2 SERVINGS • PREP TIME: 10 MINUTES**

***Nutritional Values Per Serving:*** *Calories 219; Total Fat 7g; Saturated Fat 3g; Cholesterol 47mg; Sodium 396mg; Total Carbohydrate 24g; Protein 18g*
***Food Pyramid Servings:*** *2.0 oz. Meat, Poultry, Fish, Dry Beans, Eggs & Nuts Group; 1 serving Bread, Cereal, Rice & Pasta Group; ¾ serving Vegetable Group*



Chicken Salad Sandwiches

How does your garden grow? When you serve colorfully succulent *Vegetable Tuna Toss* or *Chicken Pasta Salad*, even your littlest sprouts will cultivate an interest! For everyday or entertaining fare, put your menu plan into great shape with robust low-fat side dishes like *Vegetable-Rice Pilaf, Herbed Skillet Vegetables* and *Naturally Good Potatoes!*

Herbed Skillet Vegetables, top, (page 75) and
Garden Salad with Herb Chicken, bottom, (page 74).

# Garden Salad with Herb Chicken

1 cup refrigerated MARIE'S Zesty Fat Free Classic Herb Vinaigrette
4 skinless, boneless chicken breast halves (about 1 pound)
6 cups salad greens torn in bite-size pieces
1 large tomato, cut into 8 wedges
½ cup sliced cucumber
¼ cup sliced green onions (about 2)

• Pour *½ cup* vinaigrette into shallow nonmetallic dish. Add chicken and turn to coat. Cover and refrigerate 1 hour, turning chicken occasionally.

• Remove chicken from marinade and place on rack in broiler pan. Broil 4 inches from heat 15 minutes or until chicken is no longer pink, turning and brushing with marinade halfway through cooking. Discard remaining marinade. Slice chicken into thin strips.

• Arrange greens, tomato, cucumber, onions and chicken on 4 plates. Serve with remaining dressing. If desired, garnish with *yellow cherry tomatoes.*

**Makes 4 servings • Prep Time: 15 minutes • Marinating Time: 1 hour • Cook Time: 15 minutes**

***Nutritional Values Per Serving:*** *Calories 231; Total Fat 4g; Saturated Fat 1g; Cholesterol 74mg; Sodium 574mg; Total Carbohydrate 20g; Protein 29g*
***Food Pyramid Servings:*** *3.0 oz. Meat, Poultry, Fish, Dry Beans, Eggs & Nuts Group; 2¼ servings Vegetable Group*

# Creamy Green Beans

1 can (10¾ ounces) CAMPBELL'S HEALTHY REQUEST condensed Cream of Mushroom Soup
¼ cup milk (2% fat)
1 teaspoon soy sauce
⅛ teaspoon garlic powder
Generous dash pepper
3 cups frozen cut green beans
2 tablespoons toasted sliced almonds

• In medium saucepan mix soup, milk, soy sauce, garlic powder, pepper and beans. Over medium heat, heat to a boil. Reduce heat to low. Cover and cook 10 minutes or until beans are tender, stirring occasionally. Sprinkle with almonds.

**Makes about 3 cups or 6 servings • Prep Time: 5 minutes • Cook Time: 15 minutes**

***Nutritional Values Per Serving:*** *Calories 73; Total Fat 3g; Saturated Fat 1g; Cholesterol 2mg; Sodium 279mg; Total Carbohydrate 11g; Protein 3g*
***Food Pyramid Servings:*** *1 serving Vegetable Group*

# Herbed Skillet Vegetables

2 tablespoons cornstarch
1 can (14½ ounces) SWANSON NATURAL GOODNESS Chicken Broth
½ teaspoon dried thyme leaves, crushed
⅛ teaspoon pepper
4 cups small new potatoes cut in quarters (about 1¼ pounds)
1 cup carrots cut in 1-inch pieces (about 2 medium)
1½ cups celery cut in 2-inch pieces (about 2 ribs)

- In cup mix cornstarch and *¼ cup* broth until smooth. Set aside.
- In medium skillet mix remaining broth, thyme, pepper, potatoes, carrots and celery. Over medium-high heat, heat to a boil. Reduce heat to low. Cover and cook 20 minutes or until vegetables are tender. With slotted spoon, remove vegetables to serving dish.
- Stir reserved cornstarch mixture and add. Cook until mixture boils and thickens, stirring constantly. Serve over vegetables.

**Makes about 5½ cups or 4 servings • Prep Time: 15 minutes • Cook Time: 30 minutes**

***Nutritional Values Per Serving:*** *Calories 213; Total Fat 1g; Saturated Fat 0g; Cholesterol 0mg; Sodium 330mg; Total Carbohydrate 48g; Protein 5g*
***Food Pyramid Servings:*** *2¾ servings Vegetable Group*

# Creamy Vegetable Combo

1 can (10¾ ounces) CAMPBELL'S HEALTHY REQUEST condensed Cream of Celery Soup
½ cup milk (2% fat)
2 teaspoons lemon juice
⅛ teaspoon pepper
1 bag (16 ounces) frozen vegetable combination (broccoli, cauliflower, carrots)

- In medium saucepan mix soup, milk, lemon juice, pepper and vegetables. Over medium heat, heat to a boil.
- Reduce heat to low. Cover and cook 10 minutes or until vegetables are tender, stirring occasionally.

**Makes about 3 cups or 6 servings • Prep Time: 5 minutes • Cook Time: 15 minutes**

***Nutritional Values Per Serving:*** *Calories 60; Total Fat 1g; Saturated Fat 1g; Cholesterol 2mg; Sodium 229mg; Total Carbohydrate 10g; Protein 3g*
***Food Pyramid Servings:*** *1 serving Vegetable Group*

# Chicken Pasta Salad

- 1 can (10¾ ounces) CAMPBELL'S HEALTHY REQUEST condensed Cream of Celery Soup
- ½ cup plain low-fat yogurt
- ¼ cup water
- 2 tablespoons Dijon-style mustard
- 1 tablespoon vinegar
- ⅛ teaspoon pepper
- 4 cups cooked corkscrew macaroni (about 3 cups dry), cooked without salt
- 1 cup sliced celery (about 2 ribs)
- 1 cup diced tomato (about 1 medium)
- 2 cups cubed cooked chicken

• In small bowl mix soup, yogurt, water, mustard, vinegar and pepper.

• In large bowl toss macaroni, celery, tomato, chicken and soup mixture until evenly coated. Refrigerate at least 3 hours. If desired, line bowl with salad greens and garnish with *fresh sprouts.*

**MAKES ABOUT 7½ CUPS OR 6 SERVINGS • PREP TIME: 25 MINUTES • CHILL TIME: 3 HOURS**

***Nutritional Values Per Serving:*** *Calories 272; Total Fat 5g; Saturated Fat 2g; Cholesterol 40mg; Sodium 390mg; Total Carbohydrate 34g; Protein 19g*
***Food Pyramid Servings:*** *1.5 oz. Meat, Poultry, Fish, Dry Beans, Eggs & Nuts Group; 1⅓ servings Bread, Cereal, Rice & Pasta Group; ⅔ serving Vegetable Group*

# Vegetable Tuna Toss

- ¾ cup refrigerated MARIE'S Zesty Fat Free Red Wine Vinaigrette
- 1 cup fresh broccoli flowerets
- 1 cup carrot cut in 2-inch matchstick-thin strips (about 1 large)
- 1 cup cauliflower flowerets
- 1 cup sliced cucumber
- 1 cup cherry tomatoes cut in half
- ½ cup VLASIC *or* EARLY CALIFORNIA pitted Ripe Olives
- 2 cans (about 6 ounces *each*) tuna packed in water, drained and flaked
- ¼ cup walnuts, toasted (optional)

• Toss vinaigrette, broccoli, carrot, cauliflower, cucumber, tomatoes, olives and tuna until evenly coated. Refrigerate at least 1 hour. Stir in walnuts.

**MAKES ABOUT 8 CUPS OR 6 SERVINGS • PREP TIME: 15 MINUTES • CHILL TIME: 1 HOUR**

***Nutritional Values Per Serving:*** *Calories 161; Total Fat 5g; Saturated Fat 1g; Cholesterol 14mg; Sodium 539mg; Total Carbohydrate 16g; Protein 14g*
***Food Pyramid Servings:*** *2.0 oz. Meat, Poultry, Fish, Dry Beans, Eggs & Nuts Group; 1⅔ servings Vegetable Group*



Chicken Pasta Salad

# Oriental Beef Salad

- 2/3 cup refrigerated MARIE'S Zesty Fat Free Red Wine Vinaigrette
- 1 tablespoon soy sauce
- 1 teaspoon sesame oil (optional)
- 2 cups sliced fresh mushrooms (about 6 ounces)
- 1 cup sweet yellow, red *or* green pepper cut in 2-inch-long strips (about 1 small)
- 1/4 cup sliced green onions (about 2)
- 3/4 pound boneless beef top round steak, 1 inch thick
- 4 cups salad greens torn in bite-size pieces

• In small bowl mix vinaigrette, soy sauce and oil. Reserve 2 tablespoons.

• Add mushrooms, pepper and onions to remaining vinaigrette mixture. Toss until coated. Set aside.

• Brush both sides of steak with reserved vinaigrette mixture. Place steak on rack in broiler pan. Broil 4 inches from heat to desired doneness (allow 20 minutes for medium), turning once. Slice meat into thin strips.

• Arrange greens, mushrooms, pepper, onions and steak on 4 plates.

**MAKES 4 SERVINGS • PREP TIME: 15 MINUTES • COOK TIME: 20 MINUTES**

***Nutritional Values Per Serving:*** *Calories 199; Total Fat 5g; Saturated Fat 1g; Cholesterol 53mg; Sodium 660mg; Total Carbohydrate 17g; Protein 22g*
***Food Pyramid Servings:*** *2.0 oz. Meat, Poultry, Fish, Dry Beans, Eggs & Nuts Group; 2½ servings Vegetable Group*

# Vegetable-Rice Pilaf

- 2 teaspoons margarine
- 3/4 cup uncooked regular long-grain rice
- 1 can (14½ ounces) SWANSON Vegetable Broth
- 1/4 teaspoon dried basil leaves, crushed
- 3/4 cup frozen mixed vegetables
- 1/4 cup chopped green *or* sweet red pepper

• In medium saucepan over medium heat, heat margarine. Add rice and cook 30 seconds, stirring constantly. Stir in broth and basil. Heat to a boil. Reduce heat to low. Cover and cook 10 minutes.

• Add mixed vegetables and pepper. Cover and cook 10 minutes more or until rice is done and most of liquid is absorbed.

**MAKES ABOUT 3½ CUPS OR 4 SERVINGS • PREP TIME: 5 MINUTES • COOK TIME: 25 MINUTES**

***Nutritional Values Per Serving:*** *Calories 176; Total Fat 3g; Saturated Fat 0g; Cholesterol 0mg; Sodium 470mg; Total Carbohydrate 34g; Protein 4g*
***Food Pyramid Servings:*** *1 serving Bread, Cereal, Rice & Pasta Group; ½ serving Vegetable Group*

# Fiesta Rice

Vegetable cooking spray
½ cup chopped green pepper (about 1 small)
¼ cup chopped onion (about 1 small)
3 cups V8 Picante Vegetable Juice
¼ teaspoon garlic powder
1 cup uncooked regular long-grain rice
¼ cup shredded Monterey Jack cheese (1 ounce)

• Spray medium saucepan with cooking spray and heat over medium heat 1 minute. Add pepper and onion and cook until tender-crisp.

• Add "V8" juice, garlic powder and rice. Heat to a boil. Reduce heat to low. Cover and cook 20 minutes or until rice is done and most of liquid is absorbed. Stir in cheese. If desired, garnish with *celery leaves.*

**MAKES 4 CUPS OR 4 SERVINGS • PREP TIME: 10 MINUTES • COOK TIME: 30 MINUTES**

***Nutritional Values Per Serving:*** *Calories 242; Total Fat 3g; Saturated Fat 2g; Cholesterol 6mg; Sodium 542mg; Total Carbohydrate 46g; Protein 7g*
***Food Pyramid Servings:*** *1½ servings Bread, Cereal, Rice & Pasta Group; 1¼ servings Vegetable Group*

# Pasta Vegetable Skillet

1 tablespoon vegetable oil
3 cups sliced zucchini (about 2 medium)
1 jar (28 ounces) PREGO EXTRA CHUNKY Zesty Garlic & Cheese Spaghetti Sauce (3 cups)
4 cups cooked elbow macaroni (about 2 cups dry), cooked without salt

• In medium skillet over medium heat, heat oil. Add zucchini and cook until tender-crisp.

• Add spaghetti sauce and macaroni. Heat through, stirring occasionally.

**MAKES ABOUT 6 CUPS OR 6 SERVINGS • PREP TIME: 15 MINUTES • COOK TIME: 15 MINUTES**

***Nutritional Values Per Serving:*** *Calories 279; Total Fat 5g; Saturated Fat 1g; Cholesterol 2mg; Sodium 587mg; Total Carbohydrate 51g; Protein 8g*
***Food Pyramid Servings:*** *1⅓ servings Bread, Cereal, Rice & Pasta Group; 2 servings Vegetable Group*



Fiesta Rice

# Spaghetti Florentine

Vegetable cooking spray
½ cup chopped onion (about 1 medium)
3 cloves garlic, minced
1 teaspoon Italian seasoning, crushed
1 can (10¾ ounces) CAMPBELL'S HEALTHY REQUEST condensed Cream of Celery Soup
1 package (about 10 ounces) frozen chopped spinach
⅛ teaspoon pepper
1 cup plain low-fat yogurt
1 cup diced tomato (about 1 medium)
4 cups hot cooked spaghetti (about 8 ounces dry), cooked without salt
2 tablespoons grated Parmesan cheese

• Spray medium saucepan with cooking spray and heat over medium heat 1 minute. Add onion, garlic and Italian seasoning and cook until tender, stirring often.

• Add soup, spinach and pepper. Heat to a boil. Reduce heat to low. Cover and cook 10 minutes or until spinach is tender, breaking up spinach with fork and stirring occasionally.

• Add yogurt and tomato and heat through. Toss with spaghetti. Sprinkle with cheese. If desired, garnish with *tomatoes* and *fresh oregano.*

**MAKES ABOUT 6 CUPS OR 6 SERVINGS • PREP TIME: 10 MINUTES • COOK TIME: 25 MINUTES**

***Nutritional Values Per Serving:*** *Calories 324; Total Fat 4g; Saturated Fat 2g; Cholesterol 7mg; Sodium 459mg; Total Carbohydrate 57g; Protein 15g*
***Food Pyramid Servings:*** *2 servings Bread, Cereal, Rice & Pasta Group; 1½ servings Vegetable Group; ¼ serving Milk, Yogurt & Cheese Group*

# Naturally Good Potatoes

1 can (14½ ounces) SWANSON NATURAL GOODNESS Chicken Broth
Generous dash pepper
1⅓ cups instant mashed potato flakes *or* buds

• In medium saucepan over medium-high heat, heat broth and pepper to a boil. Stir in potato flakes.

**MAKES ABOUT 2 CUPS OR 4 SERVINGS • PREP TIME: 5 MINUTES • COOK TIME: 10 MINUTES**

***Nutritional Values Per Serving:*** *Calories 62; Total Fat 0g; Saturated Fat 0g; Cholesterol 0mg; Sodium 299mg; Total Carbohydrate 13g; Protein 2g*
***Food Pyramid Servings:*** *1 serving Vegetable Group*

# Sensibly Delicious Snacks

Today, when it comes to eating right, let Campbell's take the lead! Daringly delicious *Glazed Carrot Raisin Cupcakes, Cinnamon-Raisin Loaves* and *Colorburst Olive Pizza Slices* are just a few of the slimmed-down snack and sweet-tooth recipes that are sure to please! And, see for yourself how versatile "V8" vegetable juice charts a refresher course for smooth and sumptuous sipping!

Clockwise from top left: Glazed Carrot Raisin Cupcakes (page 87), Vegetable Tortilla Triangles (page 86) and Southwest Refresher (page 86).

## Vegetable Tortilla Triangles

- 1 can (10¾ ounces) CAMPBELL'S HEALTHY REQUEST condensed Cream of Celery Soup
- 1 cup chopped tomato (about 1 medium)
- ½ cup chopped green pepper (about 1 small)
- ¼ cup sliced green onions (about 2)
- 1 fresh *or* canned jalapeño pepper, seeded and finely chopped (about 1 tablespoon), optional
- 8 flour tortillas (8 inches *each*)
- 1 cup shredded Cheddar cheese (4 ounces)

• Mix soup, tomato, green pepper, onions and jalapeño pepper.

• Place tortillas on 2 large baking sheets. Top each tortilla with *⅓ cup* soup mixture. Spread to within ½ inch of edge. Top with cheese.

• Bake at 400°F. for 10 minutes or until tortillas are crisp. Cut each into quarters. If desired, garnish with *fresh chili peppers.*

**MAKES 32 APPETIZERS • PREP TIME: 15 MINUTES • COOK TIME: 10 MINUTES**

***Nutritional Values Per Appetizer:*** *Calories 50; Total Fat 2g; Saturated Fat 1g; Cholesterol 4mg; Sodium 105mg; Total Carbohydrate 6g; Protein 2g*
***Food Pyramid Servings:*** *¼ serving Bread, Cereal, Rice & Pasta Group*

## Southwest Refresher

- 4 cups V8 Picante Vegetable Juice, chilled
- ⅛ teaspoon chili powder
- ⅛ teaspoon ground cumin (optional)

• Mix "V8" juice, chili powder and cumin. Serve over ice cubes. If desired, garnish with *lemon peel.*

**MAKES 4 CUPS OR 6 SERVINGS • PREP TIME: 5 MINUTES**

***Nutritional Values Per Serving:*** *Calories 37; Total Fat 0g; Saturated Fat 0g; Cholesterol 0mg; Sodium 446mg; Total Carbohydrate 7g; Protein 1g*
***Food Pyramid Servings:*** *1 serving Vegetable Group*

# Glazed Carrot Raisin Cupcakes

1 package (about 18 ounces) spice cake mix
1 can (10¾ ounces) CAMPBELL'S HEALTHY REQUEST condensed Tomato Soup
½ cup water
2 eggs
½ cup shredded carrot (about 1 medium)
½ cup raisins
1 cup confectioners' sugar
3 tablespoons unsweetened apple juice

- Preheat oven to 350°F. Place liners in twenty-four 2½-inch muffin-pan cups.
- Mix cake mix, soup, water and eggs according to package directions. Fold in carrot and raisins. Spoon batter into muffin cups, filling almost full.
- Bake 20 minutes or until toothpick inserted in center of cupcakes comes out clean. Remove cupcakes from pan and cool completely.
- Mix sugar and juice until smooth. Frost cupcakes. If desired, serve with *fresh fruit.*

**MAKES 24 SERVINGS • PREP TIME: 10 MINUTES • COOK TIME: 20 MINUTES**

***Nutritional Values Per Serving:*** *Calories 124; Total Fat 2g; Saturated Fat 0g; Cholesterol 18mg; Sodium 182mg; Total Carbohydrate 24g; Protein 1g*
***Food Pyramid Servings:*** *1 serving Bread, Cereal, Rice & Pasta Group*

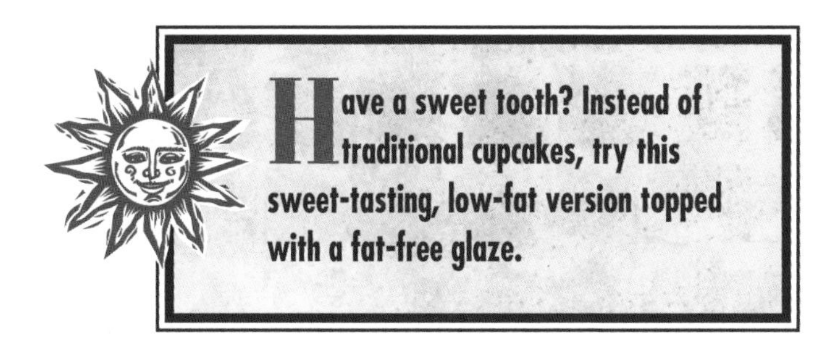

# Curried Chicken Spread

- 3 tablespoons nonfat mayonnaise dressing
- 3 tablespoons chopped chutney
- ¼ teaspoon curry powder
- 1 can (5 ounces) SWANSON Premium Chunk White *or* Chunk Chicken, drained
- ½ cup chopped tart apple
- 1 tablespoon chopped, unsalted dry roasted peanuts

• Mix mayonnaise, chutney, curry powder, chicken, apple and peanuts. If desired, garnish with *apple slices* and *fresh mint.*

**MAKES ABOUT 1¼ CUPS OR 10 SERVINGS • PREP TIME: 10 MINUTES**

***Nutritional Values Per Serving (2 Tablespoons):*** *Calories 37; Total Fat 1g; Saturated Fat 0g; Cholesterol 7mg; Sodium 103mg; Total Carbohydrate 5g; Protein 3g*
***Food Pyramid Servings:*** *0.5 oz. Meat, Poultry, Fish, Dry Beans, Eggs & Nuts Group*

# Mexican Bean Dip

- 1 can (11½ ounces) CAMPBELL'S HEALTHY REQUEST condensed Bean with Bacon Soup
- ½ cup plain nonfat yogurt
- 1 teaspoon chili powder
- ¼ teaspoon garlic powder
- ¾ cup cut-up canned tomatoes
- 1 tablespoon chopped green onion

• Mix soup, yogurt, chili powder, garlic powder, tomatoes and onion. If desired, garnish with *green onions.*

**MAKES ABOUT 2 CUPS OR 16 SERVINGS • PREP TIME: 10 MINUTES**

***Nutritional Values Per Serving (2 Tablespoons):*** *Calories 32; Total Fat 1g; Saturated Fat 0g; Cholesterol 1mg; Sodium 104mg; Total Carbohydrate 5g; Protein 2g*
***Food Pyramid Servings:*** *¼ serving Vegetable Group*

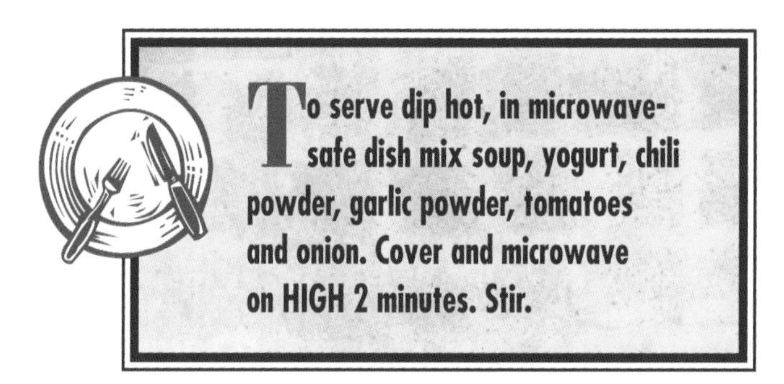


Curried Chicken Spread (*top*)
Mexican Bean Dip (*bottom*)

# Orange V8 Spritzer

- 3 cups Low Sodium V8 Vegetable Juice, chilled
- 1½ cups plain *or* orange-flavored seltzer water, chilled
- ¼ cup orange juice

• Mix "V8" juice, seltzer and orange juice. Serve over ice cubes. If desired, garnish with *cucumber slices* and *carrot sticks.*

**Makes about 4¾ cups or 6 servings • Prep Time: 5 minutes**

***Nutritional Values Per Serving:*** *Calories 36; Total Fat 0g; Saturated Fat 0g; Cholesterol 0mg; Sodium 82mg; Total Carbohydrate 8g; Protein 1g*
***Food Pyramid Servings:*** *⅔ serving Vegetable Group*

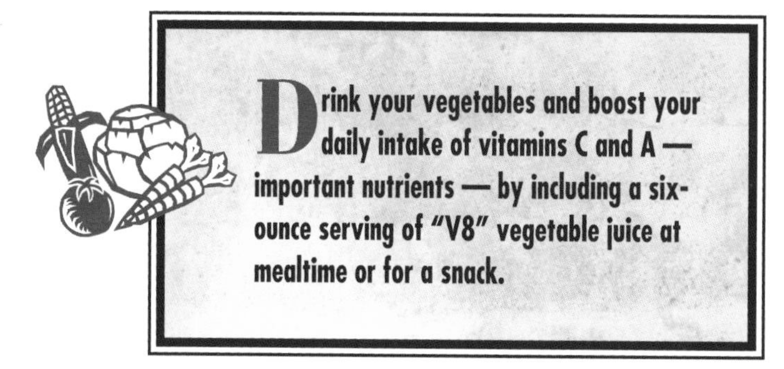

**Drink your vegetables and boost your daily intake of vitamins C and A — important nutrients — by including a six-ounce serving of "V8" vegetable juice at mealtime or for a snack.**

# Colorburst Olive Pizza Slices

- 1 loaf (about 14 ounces) Italian bread (about 16 inches long), cut lengthwise
- ⅓ cup refrigerated MARIE'S reduced calorie Creamy Italian Garlic Dressing
- 1 cup chopped green, sweet red *and/or* yellow pepper (about 1 medium)
- ¼ cup sliced green onions (about 2)
- ¼ cup sliced VLASIC *or* EARLY CALIFORNIA pitted Ripe Olives
- ¾ cup shredded part-skim mozzarella cheese (3 ounces)

• Bake bread on baking sheet at 400°F. for 5 minutes or until lightly toasted. Spread dressing on bread. Top with peppers, onions, olives and cheese. Bake 10 minutes more or until cheese is melted. Cut each bread half into 12 slices.

**Makes 24 appetizers • Prep Time: 15 minutes • Cook Time: 15 minutes**

***Nutritional Values Per Appetizer:*** *Calories 71; Total Fat 2g; Saturated Fat 1g; Cholesterol 3mg; Sodium 180mg; Total Carbohydrate 10g; Protein 3g*
***Food Pyramid Servings:*** *½ serving Bread, Cereal, Rice & Pasta Group*

Orange V8 Spritzer (*top*)
Colorburst Olive Pizza Slices (*bottom*)

# Cinnamon-Raisin Loaves

- Vegetable cooking spray
- 3 cups all-purpose flour
- 2 teaspoons ground cinnamon
- 1 teaspoon baking soda
- ½ teaspoon baking powder
- 1½ cups sugar
- 1 can (10¾ ounces) CAMPBELL'S HEALTHY REQUEST condensed Tomato Soup
- 6 egg whites
- ⅓ cup vegetable oil
- 1 teaspoon vanilla extract
- 2 cups shredded zucchini (about 2 small)
- 1 cup raisins

• Preheat oven to 350°F. Spray two 8½- by 4½-inch loaf pans with cooking spray and set aside.

• Mix flour, cinnamon, baking soda and baking powder and set aside.

• Mix sugar, soup, egg whites, oil and vanilla. Add to flour mixture, stirring just to moisten. Fold in zucchini and raisins. Pour into prepared pans.

• Bake in center of oven 55 minutes or until toothpick inserted in center comes out clean. Cool in pans on wire rack 10 minutes. Remove from pans and cool completely. If desired, garnish with *fresh fruit* and *fresh mint.*

**MAKES 24 SERVINGS • PREP TIME: 20 MINUTES • COOK TIME: 55 MINUTES**

***Nutritional Values Per Serving:*** *Calories 170; Total Fat 3g; Saturated Fat 1g; Cholesterol 0mg; Sodium 119mg; Total Carbohydrate 32g; Protein 3g*
***Food Pyramid Servings:*** *1 serving Bread, Cereal, Rice & Pasta Group*

**Cinnamon-Raisin Squares:** Substitute 13- by 9-inch baking pan for loaf pans. Bake 40 minutes or until toothpick inserted in center comes out clean. Cool in pan on wire rack. Serves 24.

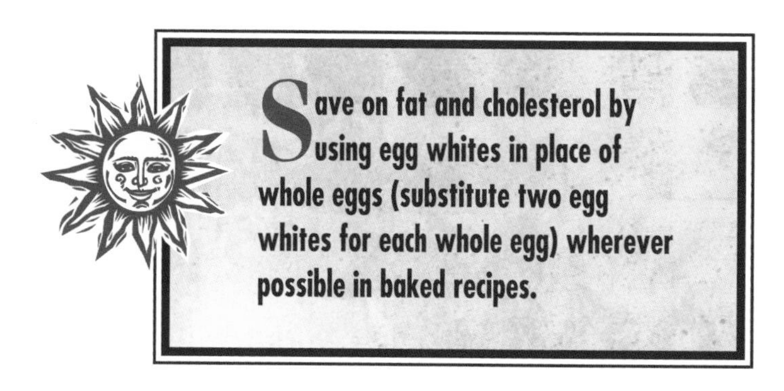

# Recipe Index

**Appetizers**
- Colorburst Olive Pizza Slices, 90
- Curried Chicken Spread, 88
- Mexican Bean Dip, 88
- Vegetable Tortilla Triangles, 86

Barbecued Chicken Sandwiches, 66
Barbecued Turkey Pockets, 18
**Beef (*see also* Ground Beef)**
- Beef and Broccoli Stir-Fry, 48
- Beef and Mushrooms Dijon, 46
- Oriental Beef Salad, 78
- Piquant Pot Roast, 23
- Quick and Easy Swiss Steak, 52
- Skillet Beef Oriental, 50

**Beverages**
- Orange V8 Spritzer, 90
- Southwest Refresher, 86

Broccoli Fish Bake, 42

**Chicken**
- Barbecued Chicken Sandwiches, 66
- Chicken and Bean Burritos, 68
- Chicken and Broccoli Pockets, 66
- Chicken Broccoli Twist, 12
- Chicken Pasta Salad, 76
- Chicken Primavera, 24
- Chicken Quesadillas, 62
- Chicken Salad Sandwiches, 70
- Chicken "Stir-Fry", 22
- Chicken Tetrazzini with a Twist, 34
- Curried Chicken Chowder, 64
- Curried Chicken Spread, 88
- Easy Italian Chicken Bake, 14
- Easy Lemon Chicken, 32
- Garden Salad with Herb Chicken, 74
- Herb Broiled Chicken, 30
- Herbed Brown Rice and Chicken, 36
- Herbed Chicken Vegetable Sauté, 28
- Honey-Barbecued Chicken, 16
- Honey-Mustard Chicken, 38
- Italian Chicken and Shells, 26
- Lemon Thyme Chicken Crunch, 30
- Mexican Chicken Soup, 60
- Oriental Chicken Sandwiches, 70
- Savory Lemon Chicken, 26
- Skillet Basil Chicken, 38
- Spicy Barbecued Chicken, 28
- Zesty Chicken Fajitas, 57

Chill-Chasing Chili, 13
Cinnamon-Raisin Loaves, 92
Cinnamon-Raisin Squares, 92
Colorburst Olive Pizza Slices, 90
Corny Mac 'n' Beef, 14
Creamy Green Beans, 74
Creamy Potato Soup, 58
Creamy Vegetable Combo, 75
Curried Chicken Chowder, 64
Curried Chicken Spread, 88

**Desserts**
- Cinnamon-Raisin Loaves, 92
- Cinnamon-Raisin Squares, 92
- Glazed Carrot Raisin Cupcakes, 87

Easy Italian Chicken Bake, 14
Easy Lemon Chicken, 32

Fiesta Rice, 80
Food Guide Pyramid, 4

Garden Salad with Herb Chicken, 74
Glazed Carrot Raisin Cupcakes, 87
**Ground Beef (*see also* Beef)**
- Chill-Chasing Chili, 13
- Corny Mac 'n' Beef, 14
- Souperburgers, 18

Harvest Pork 'n' Noodles, 52
Hearty Tomato Rice Soup, 64
Hearty Vegetable Soup, 68
Herb Broiled Chicken, 30
Herbed Brown Rice and Chicken, 36
Herbed Chicken Vegetable Sauté, 28
Herbed Skillet Vegetables, 75
Honey-Barbecued Chicken, 16
Honey-Mustard Chicken, 38

Italian Chicken and Shells, 26
Italiano Turkey and Pasta, 40
Italian Vegetable Soup, 60

Lemon Thyme Chicken Crunch, 30
Low-Fat Cooking Tips, 9
Low-Fat Snacking Tips, 9

Mac 'n' Vegetable Soup, 58

# Recipe Index continued


Mexican Bean Dip, 88
Mexican Chicken Soup, 60

Naturally Good Potatoes, 82

Orange V8 Spritzer, 90
Oriental Beef Salad, 78
Oriental Chicken Sandwiches, 70

**Pasta**
- Chicken Broccoli Twist, 12
- Chicken Pasta Salad, 76
- Chicken Primavera, 24
- Chicken Tetrazzini with a Twist, 34
- Corny Mac 'n' Beef, 14
- Italian Chicken and Shells, 26
- Italiano Turkey and Pasta, 40
- Pasta Vegetable Skillet, 80
- Spaghetti Florentine, 82
- Spicy Cheese Twisters, 16
- Piquant Pot Roast, 23

**Pork**
- Harvest Pork 'n' Noodles, 52
- Smothered Pork Chops, 50

Quick and Easy Swiss Steak, 52

**Salads**
- Chicken Pasta Salad, 76
- Garden Salad with Herb Chicken, 74
- Oriental Beef Salad, 78
- Vegetable Tuna Toss, 76

**Sandwiches**
- Barbecued Chicken Sandwiches, 66
- Barbecued Turkey Pockets, 18
- Chicken and Bean Burritos, 68
- Chicken and Broccoli Pockets, 66
- Chicken Quesadillas, 62
- Chicken Salad Sandwiches, 70
- Oriental Chicken Sandwiches, 70
- Souperburgers, 18
- Zesty Chicken Fajitas, 57

Savory Lemon Chicken, 26

**Seafood**
- Broccoli Fish Bake, 42
- Shrimp Stir-Fry, 44

**Side Dishes**
- Creamy Green Beans, 74
- Creamy Vegetable Combo, 75
- Fiesta Rice, 80
- Herbed Skillet Vegetables, 75
- Naturally Good Potatoes, 82
- Pasta Vegetable Skillet, 80
- Spaghetti Florentine, 82
- Vegetable-Rice Pilaf, 78
- Vegetables 'n' Taters, 13

Skillet Basil Chicken, 38
Skillet Beef Oriental, 50
Smart and Sensible Eating Tips, 4-9
Smothered Pork Chops, 50
Souperburgers, 18

**Soups**
- Creamy Potato Soup, 58
- Curried Chicken Chowder, 64
- Hearty Tomato Rice Soup, 64
- Hearty Vegetable Soup, 68
- Italian Vegetable Soup, 60
- Mac 'n' Vegetable Soup, 58
- Mexican Chicken Soup, 60
- Tortellini Soup, 62
- Vegetarian Chili, 56

Southwest Refresher, 86
Spaghetti Florentine, 82
Spicy Barbecued Chicken, 28
Spicy Cheese Twisters, 16

Tortellini Soup, 62

**Turkey**
- Barbecued Turkey Pockets, 18
- Italiano Turkey and Pasta, 40

Vegetable-Rice Pilaf, 78
Vegetable Tortilla Triangles, 86
Vegetable Tuna Toss, 76

**Vegetables**
- Creamy Green Beans, 74
- Creamy Vegetable Combo, 75
- Herbed Skillet Vegetables, 75
- Naturally Good Potatoes, 82
- Vegetables 'n' Taters, 13

Vegetarian Chili, 56

Zesty Chicken Fajitas, 57

# Recipes By Product Index

**CAMPBELL'S CONDENSED SOUPS**
Chicken Broth
Herb Broiled Chicken, 30

HEALTHY REQUEST Bean with Bacon Soup
Chicken and Bean Burritos, 68
Mexican Bean Dip, 88

HEALTHY REQUEST Chicken with Rice Soup
Curried Chicken Chowder, 64

HEALTHY REQUEST Cream of Broccoli Soup
Broccoli Fish Bake, 42
Chicken Broccoli Twist, 12
Easy Lemon Chicken, 32
Herbed Chicken Vegetable Sauté, 28

HEALTHY REQUEST Cream of Celery Soup
Chicken Pasta Salad, 76
Creamy Vegetable Combo, 75
Harvest Pork 'n' Noodles, 52
Souperburgers, 18
Spaghetti Florentine, 82
Vegetable Tortilla Triangles, 86
Vegetables 'n' Taters, 13

HEALTHY REQUEST Cream of Chicken Soup
Chicken and Broccoli Pockets, 66
Chicken Quesadillas, 62
Curried Chicken Chowder, 64
Lemon Thyme Chicken Crunch, 30
Savory Lemon Chicken, 26
Spicy Cheese Twisters, 16

HEALTHY REQUEST Cream of Mushroom Soup
Beef and Mushrooms Dijon, 46
Chicken Tetrazzini with a Twist, 34
Creamy Green Beans, 74
Skillet Basil Chicken, 38
Skillet Beef Oriental, 50

HEALTHY REQUEST Tomato Soup
Barbecued Turkey Pockets, 18
Chill-Chasing Chili, 13
Cinnamon-Raisin Loaves, 92
Cinnamon-Raisin Squares, 92
Corny Mac 'n' Beef, 14
Easy Italian Chicken Bake, 14
Glazed Carrot Raisin Cupcakes, 87
Hearty Tomato Rice Soup, 64
Spicy Barbecued Chicken, 28

Tomato Soup
Honey-Barbecued Chicken, 16

**MARIE'S DRESSING AND VINAIGRETTES**
Colorburst Olive Pizza Slices, 90
Garden Salad with Herb Chicken, 74
Oriental Beef Salad, 78
Vegetable Tuna Toss, 76
Zesty Chicken Fajitas, 57

**PACE THICK & CHUNKY SALSA**
Chicken and Bean Burritos, 68

**PEPPERIDGE FARM BREADS**
Chicken Salad Sandwiches, 70
Oriental Chicken Sandwiches, 70

**PREGO EXTRA CHUNKY SPAGHETTI SAUCES**
Italiano Turkey and Pasta, 40
Pasta Vegetable Skillet, 80

**SWANSON BROTHS**
Beef and Broccoli Stir-Fry, 48
Chicken Primavera, 24
Creamy Potato Soup, 58
Hearty Vegetable Soup, 68
Italian Chicken and Shells, 26
Mac 'n' Vegetable Soup, 58
Quick and Easy Swiss Steak, 52
Smothered Pork Chops, 50
Vegetable-Rice Pilaf, 78
Vegetarian Chili, 56

**SWANSON CHUNK CHICKEN**
Barbecued Chicken Sandwiches, 66
Chicken Broccoli Twist, 12
Chicken Primavera, 24
Chicken Quesadillas, 62
Chicken Salad Sandwiches, 70
Chicken Tetrazzini with a Twist, 34
Curried Chicken Chowder, 64
Curried Chicken Spread, 88
Oriental Chicken Sandwiches, 70

**SWANSON NATURAL GOODNESS BROTH**
Chicken Broccoli Twist, 12
Chicken "Stir-Fry", 22
Herbed Brown Rice and Chicken, 36
Herbed Skillet Vegetables, 75
Honey-Mustard Chicken, 38
Italian Vegetable Soup, 60
Mexican Chicken Soup, 60
Naturally Good Potatoes, 82
Shrimp Stir-Fry, 44
Tortellini Soup, 62

**V8 VEGETABLE JUICES**
Fiesta Rice, 80
Orange V8 Spritzer, 90
Piquant Pot Roast, 23
Southwest Refresher, 86

**VLASIC *or* EARLY CALIFORNIA OLIVES**
Colorburst Olive Pizza Slices, 90
Vegetable Tuna Toss, 76

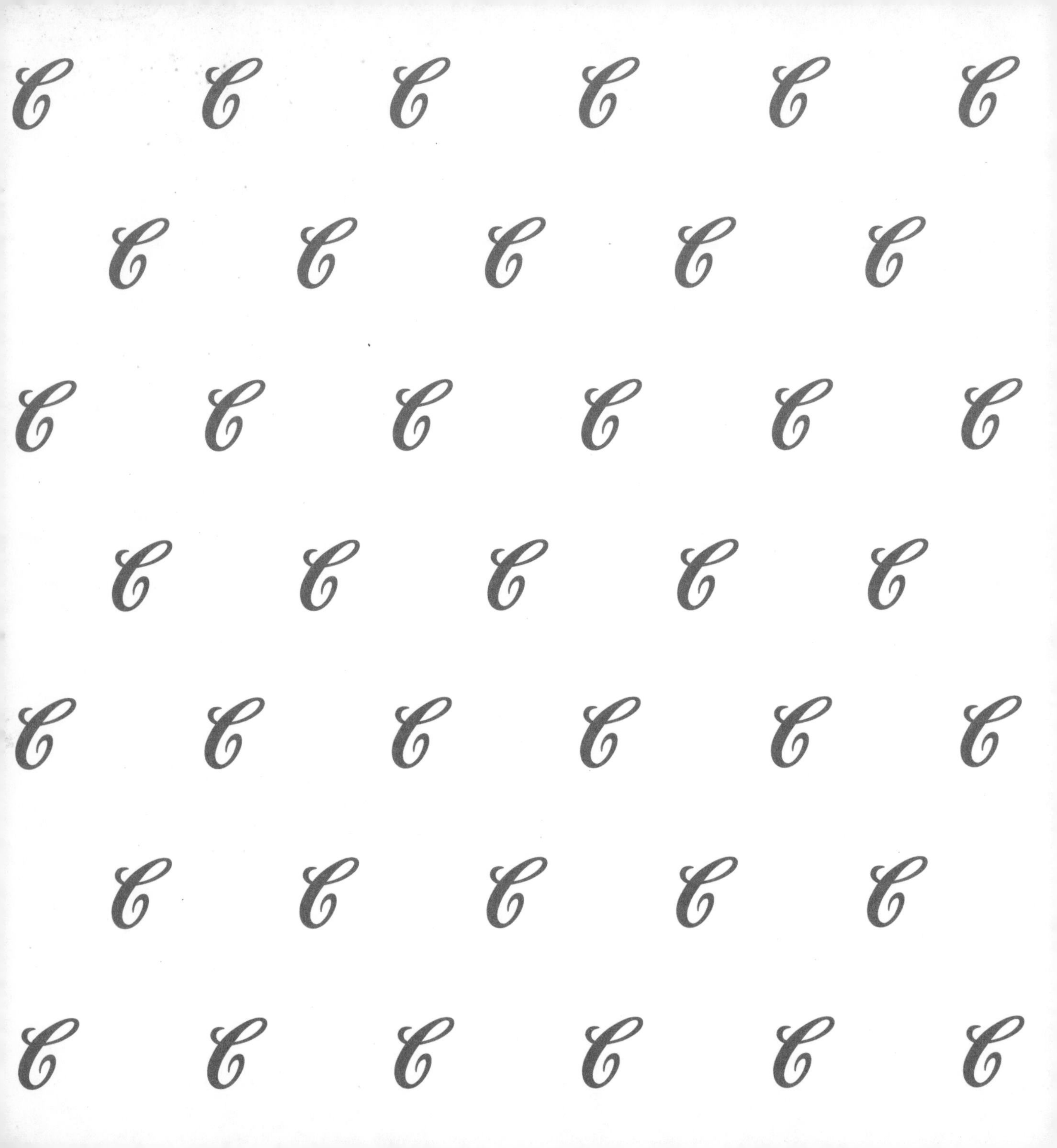